The Fourteenth Amendment
and the Bill of Rights

The
Fourteenth
Amendment
and the
Bill of Rights

By Raoul Berger

University of Oklahoma Press : Norman and London

By Raoul Berger

Congress v. The Supreme Court (Cambridge, Mass., 1969)
Impeachment: The Constitutional Problems (Cambridge, Mass.,
  1973)
Executive Privilege: A Constitutional Myth (Cambridge, Mass.,
  1974)
*Government by Judiciary: The Transformation of the Fourteenth
  Amendment* (Cambridge, Mass., 1977)
Death Penalties: The Supreme Court's Obstacle Course (Cambridge,
  Mass., 1982)
Selected Writings on the Constitution (Cumberland, W.Va., 1987)
Federalism: The Founders' Design (Norman, 1987)
The Fourteenth Amendment and the Bill of Rights (Norman, 1989)

Library of Congress Cataloging-in-Publication Data
Berger, Raoul, 1901–
The Fourteenth Amendment and the Bill of Rights.
Bibliography: p. 151.
Includes index.
  1. United States—Constitutional law—Amendments—
14th—History. 2. United States—Constitutional law—
Amendments—1st-10th—History. 3. Civil rights—United
States—History. 4. Afro-Americans—Civil rights—
History. 5. Slavery—Law and legislation—United
States—History. I. Title.
KF4757.B42   1989   342.73'085   88–40541
ISBN 0–8061–2186–6 (alk. paper)   347.30285

99189

To the memory of Lenerl

Contents

Abbreviations

Avins	Alfred Avins, *The Reconstruction Amendments' Debates* (1967)
Berger, *Judiciary*	Raoul Berger, *Government by Judiciary: The Transformation of the Fourteenth Amendment* (1977)
Berger, *Incorporation*	Raoul Berger, "Incorporation of the Bill of Rights in the Fourteenth Amendment," 42 Ohio State Law Journal 435 (1981)
Berger, *Reply*	Raoul Berger, "Incorporation of the Bill of Rights: A Reply to Michael Curtis' Response," 44 Ohio State Law Journal 1 (1983)
Bickel	Alexander Bickel, "The Original Understanding and the Segregation Decision," 69 Harvard Law Review 1 (1955)
Bond	James E. Bond, "The Original Understanding of the Fourteenth Amendment in Illinois, Ohio and Pennsylvania," 18 Akron Law Review 435 (1985)
Curtis, Book	Michael Curtis, *No State Shall Abridge the Fourteenth Amendment and the Bill of Rights* (1986)
Curtis, *Reply*	Michael Curtis, "The Bill of Rights as a Limitation on State Liberty: A

Reply to Professor Berger," 16
Wake Forest Law Review 45 (1980)

Curtis, *Adventures*   Michael Curtis. "Further
Adventures of the Nine-Lived Cat:
A Response to Mr. Berger on
Incorporation of the Bill of
Rights," 43 Ohio State Law Journal
89 (1982).

Fairman   Charles Fairman, "Does the
Fourteenth Amendment
Incorporate the Bill of Rights?" 2
Stanford Law Review 5 (1949)

Flack   Horace Flack, *The Adoption of the
Fourteenth Amendment* (1908)

Globe   Congressional Globe (39th Cong.,
1st Sess., 1866)

James   Joseph B. James, *The Framing of the
Fourteenth Amendment* (1965)

The Fourteenth Amendment
and the Bill of Rights

PART I

CHAPTER ONE

Introduction

WHETHER the Bill of Rights applies to the States by virtue of the Fourteenth Amendment presents a momentous question. For if it does not, many modern decisions of the Supreme Court—e.g., respecting First Amendment freedom of speech, Fourth Amendment search and seizure, Fifth Amendment criminal procedure, issues the Founders left to the States—are without constitutional warrant.[1] "It is difficult to imagine a more consequential subject than this one," said William van Alstyne; and it is "astonishing that the answer should be thought doubtful at this late date . . . more than a century after the ratification of the Fourteenth Amendment."[2]

That the Bill of Rights has no application to the States appears on the face of the First Amendment—"Congress shall make no law"—and is confirmed by the legislative history.[3] In proposing the First Amendment, James Madison

[1]Gerald Lynch, "Book Review," 63 Cornell L. Rev. 1091, 1094 (1978); Michael Curtis, "The Bill of Rights as a Limitation on State Authority: A Reply to Professor Berger," 16 Wake Forest L. Rev. 45, 46 (1980).

[2]William van Alstyne, "Foreword" in Michael Curtis, *No State Shall Abridge the Fourteenth Amendment and the Bill of Rights* ix (1986).

[3]"The primary purpose of the First Amendment was to reserve to the States an exclusive authority, as far as legislation was concerned, in the field of speech and press." Leonard Levy, *Judgments: Essays on American Constitutional History* 136 (1972).

urged its extension to the States because "the State governments are as liable to attack these invaluable privileges as the General Government is, and therefore ought to be cautiously guarded against."[4] But the view that finally prevailed was that of Thomas Tucker: "It will be much better, I apprehend, to leave the State Governments to themselves."[5] Egbert Benson explained that the Committee of Eleven, to whom the amendments had been referred, "meant to provide against their being infringed by the [federal] government."[6] Such was Thomas Jefferson's understanding. With respect to freedom of the press, he wrote to Abigail Adams on September 11, 1804, that

> the power is fully possessed by the several state legislatures. It was reserved to them, and was denied to the general government. . . . While we deny that Congress have a right to controul the freedom of the press, we have ever asserted the right of the States, and their exclusive right to do so.[7]

In short, "the prohibition on Congress was motivated . . . by a solicitude for states rights and the federal principle."[8]

Hence, Chief Justice John Marshall held in *Barron v. Baltimore* (1833) that the Bill of Rights had no application to the States, saying,

> Had Congress engaged in the extraordinary occupation of improving the Constitutions of the several States by affording the

[4] 1 *Annals of Congress* 441 (Gales & Seaton, 1834, print bearing running head "History of Congress").

[5] Id. 755.

[6] Id. 732.

[7] Felix Frankfurter, "John Marshall and the Judicial Function," 69 Harv. L. Rev. 217, 226 (1955).

[8] Levy, supra note 3 at 136. Referring to the "declarations of rights" proposed by the State Ratification Conventions, Madison wrote, "all of them indicat[ed] a jealousy of Federal powers, and an anxiety to multiply securities against a constructive enlargement of them." 4 *Letters and Other Writings of James Madison*, 121, 129 (1865).

people additional protection for the exercise of power by their own governments in matters which concerned themselves alone, they would have declared this purpose in plain and intelligible language.[9]

Thereby he recognized the jealous regard of the States for their sovereignty in local affairs.[10] For 135 years, Justices Harlan and Stewart reminded the Court, every member had agreed that the Founders exempted the States from the Bill of Rights.[11] This, Louis Henkin observed, was "the consistent, often reaffirmed, and almost unanimous jurisprudence of the Court."[12]

It fell to Justice Black, dissenting in *Adamson v. California* (1947), to discover in the legislative history of the Fourteenth Amendment an intention to incorporate the Bill of Rights therein.[13] Forty years have passed since *Adamson* and the Court's response is worth recounting. Addressing the privileges or immunities clause, it approved of the *Slaughter-House Cases* which, according to Justice Field, had reduced the clause to "a vain and idle enactment,"[14] and stated:

It accords with the constitutional doctrine of federalism by leaving to the states the responsibility of dealing with the privileges

[9] 32 U.S. (7 Pet.) 243, 250 (1833).

[10] Curtis recognizes that "the decision in *Barron* was a vindication of state's rights." Curtis, Book 23.

[11] Duncan v. Louisiana, 391 U.S. 145, 173 (1968).

[12] Louis Henkin, "'Selective Incorporation' in the Fourteenth Amendment," 73 Yale L.J. 74, 76 (1963).

[13] 332 U.S. 46, 80–90 (1947). The argument had been pressed upon the Court in Maxwell v. Dow, 176 U.S. 581, 587 (1899): "It is now urged in substance that all the provisions contained in the first ten amendments, so far as they secure and recognize the fundamental rights of the individual as against the exercise of federal power, are by virtue of this amendment to be regarded as privileges or immunities of a citizen of the United States." The argument failed.

[14] Slaughter-House Cases, 83 U.S. (16 Wall.) 36, 96 (1872), dissenting opinion.

and immunities of their citizens except those inherent in national citizenship.[15]

Charles Fairman, a most fastidious and careful scholar, sifted the legislative history of the Fourteenth Amendment in 1949 and published a 139-page refutation of Black's "history."[16] Alexander Bickel, the outstanding constitutional scholar of his generation, subsequently studied the legislative history and considered that Fairman's article was "conclusive."[17] And in 1959, Justice Frankfurter stated on behalf of the Court:

> We have held from the beginning and uniformly that the Due Process Clause of the Fourteenth Amendment does not apply to the States any of the provisions of the first ten amendments as such. The relevant historical materials demonstrate conclusively that Congress and the members of the legislatures of the ratifying States, did not contemplate that the Fourteenth Amendment was a shorthand incorporation of the first eight amend-

[15] Id. 53.

[16] Charles Fairman, "Does the Fourteenth Amendment Incorporate the Bill of Rights?" 2 Stan. L. Rev. 5 (1949). Leonard Levy, who lauds Curtis, infra Chapter 5 text accompanying note 4, wrote:

> Black did not merely misread history, nor wishfully attribute to it a factual content it did not possess; he mangled and manipulated it by artfully selecting facts from one side only, by generalizing from grossly inadequate "proof," by ignoring confusion and even contradictions in the minds of his key protagonists, and by assuming that silence on the part of their opponents signified acquiescence.

Levy, supra note 3 at 68.

My own study of the records in 1977 convinced me that the historical evidence confirmed Fairman. Berger, *Government by Judiciary: The Transformation of the Fourteenth Amendment* 134–156 (1977). The most recent critic of those views acknowledges that Berger's "work is representative of a broadly held scholarly view." Curtis, Book 113.

[17] Alexander Bickel, *The Least Dangerous Branch* 102 (1962)

ments making them applicable as explicit restrictions upon the States.[18]

SELECTIVE INCORPORATION

Although the Court rejected Justice Black's wholesale "incorporation," it achieved the result through the doctrine of "selective incorporation." It did not root it in the "original intention" of the framers, however, but conjured it out of the "principle[s] of justice."[19] Because "selective incorporation" purportedly derives from the due process clause, it bears emphasis that, on the eve of the Convention, Alexander Hamilton stated that those words

> have a precise technical import, and are only applicable to the process and proceedings of courts of justice; they can never be referred to an act of the legislature.[20]

My own study of four hundred years of history epitomized by Hamilton confirmed his summary.[21] But for a few aberrant cases, among them *Dred Scott,* the meaning of the Fifth Amendment's due process clause, wrote Charles Curtis,

[18] Bartkus v. Illinois, 359 U.S. 121, 124 (1959).

[19] Palko v. Connecticut, 302 U.S. 319, 325 (1925). Gressman points out that the framers "intended to incorporate those basic rights not into the Due Process Clause but into the Privileges and Immunities Clause. . . . By castrating the Privileges and Immunities Clause . . . the Supreme Court has forcibly shifted the debate into the unintended forum of the Due Process Clause . . . searching for something that the framers never really intended." Gressman, "Book Review," 1 New Law Books Reviewer 57, 59–60 (1986). Thus, like Curtis, Gressman would resuscitate the "privileges or immunities" clause from the paralyzing blow delivered by the *Slaughter-House Cases.*

[20] 4 *The Papers of Alexander Hamilton* 35 (H. Syrett & J. Cooke, eds. 1962).

[21] Raoul Berger, "'Law of the Land' Reconsidered," 74 Nw. U.L. Rev. 1 (1979).

an admirer of the Court's transformation of the words, "was as fixed and definite as the common law could make a phrase. . . . It meant a procedural process."[22]

In the Fourteenth Amendment, the Court stated, the words were "used in the same sense and with no greater extent,"[23] as the legislative history confirms. When asked what the words "due process" meant, John Bingham, draftsman of the Fourteenth Amendment, shortly replied, "the courts have settled that long ago, and the gentleman can go and read their decisions,"[24] indicating that he thought the question frivolous. Speaking to the Bingham amendment, James Wilson, chairman of the House Judiciary Committee, indicated that the due process clause furnished a "remedy" to secure the "fundamental rights enumerated in the Civil Rights Act."[25] Judge William Lawrence, a member of the thirty-ninth Congress, quoted the Hamilton procedural definition in 1871;[26] and in the same year another framer, James Garfield, said that due process of law meant "an im-

---

[22] C. Curtis, "Review and Majority Rule" in *Supreme Court and Supreme Law* 170, 177 (Edmond Cahn, ed. 1954). In a classic study, Charles G. Haines wrote that due process of law "referred in England to a method of procedure in criminal trials." C. Haines, *The American Doctrine of Judicial Supremacy* 410 (1959).

[23] Hurtado v. California, 110 U.S. 516, 535 (1894).

[24] Avins 157. Dean James Bond found that during the Ratification campaign Republicans represented that the due process clause "guaranteed only procedural fairness." J. Bond, "The Original Understanding of the Fourteenth Amendment in Illinois, Ohio, and Pennsylvania," 18 Akron L. Rev. 435, 443 (1985).

[25] Avins 189.

[26] Id. 479. Of such data Curtis takes little account, but cites instead Sumner's view that "the due process clause 'brief as it is, is in itself alone a whole Bill of Rights'." Curtis, Book 130. It is such unorthodox views that deprived Sumner of credibility in the Senate. See Raoul Berger, "The Fourteenth Amendment: Light From the Fifteenth," 74 Nw. U.L. Rev. 311, 327, 328–29 (1979).

partial trial according to the law of the land."²⁷ Dean John Hart Ely found no references in the legislative history that gave the due process clause of the Fourteenth Amendment "more than a procedural connotation,"²⁸ as I likewise found. In a searching study of selective incorporation, Louis Henkin concluded that it "finds no support in the language of the amendment, or in the history of its adoption," and that it is truly "more difficult to justify than Justice Black's position that the Bill of Rights was wholly incorporated."²⁹ Thereafter, Judge Henry Friendly regarded it as "undisputed" that "selective incorporation" has "no historical support," observing that "the present Justices feel that if their predecessors could arrange for the absorption of some such provision in the due process clause they ought to possess similar absorptive capacity toward other provisions equally important in their eyes."³⁰ "The way we arrived at incorporation," Paul Bator wrote, "was intellectually shoddy. It was just announced as though it was a *coup d'etat*; suddenly we had incorporation."³¹

It will profit us to examine the derivation of the doctrine more closely. Before "liberty of contract"—derived from the "liberty" of the due process clause—was abandoned, the

²⁷Cong. Globe, 42d Cong., 1st Sess. 153 (1871); Avins 529. Lysander Spooner and Joel Tiffany, two leading abolitionist theorists, "refused to rely on due process" or "thought of it almost entirely as a formal requirement." Jacobus tenBroek, *Equal Under Law* 121 (1965).

²⁸J. H. Ely, "Constitutional Interpretivism: Its Allure and Impossibility," 53 Ind. L.J. 399, 416 (1978).

²⁹Louis Henkin, "'Selective Incorporation' in the Fourteenth Amendment," 73 Yale L.J. 74, 77 (1963). "There is no evidence, and it is difficult to conceive, that any one thought or intended that the amendment would impose on the states a selective incorporation." Id. 77–78.

³⁰H. Friendly, "The Bill of Rights as a Code of Criminal Procedure," 53 Calif. L. Rev. 929, 935 (1965).

³¹Paul Bator, "Some Thoughts on Applied Federalism," 6 Harv. J. of Law & Pub. Policy 51, 58 (1982). See Levy, *infra* text accompanying note 34.

Justices timidly extended the concept to freedom of speech. As late as 1922 the Court had held that the Constitution "imposes upon the States no obligation to confer upon those within their jurisdiction . . . the right of free speech."[32] Three years later, in *Gitlow v. New York,* the Court "*assume[d]* that freedom of speech and of the press—which are protected by the first amendment from abridgement by *Congress*—are among the fundamental personal rights and 'liberties' protected by the due process clause of the fourteenth amendment from impairment by the States."[33] Commenting on the shift, Leonard Levy observed, "Judicial behavior is sometimes inexplicable. . . . Thus casually and without reasoned judgment, and despite precedents to the contrary, the Court began a process of incorporating selected provisions of the Bill of Rights into the due process clause."[34] Justice Holmes furnished the clue in his dissenting *Gitlow* opinion: free speech "must be taken to be included in the Fourteenth Amendments *in view of the scope that has been given* to the word 'liberty' as there used."[35] But this was precarious footing. Charles Warren tellingly pointed out that the "free speech" of the First Amendment could not have been comprehended in the due process of the Fifth because "having already provided in the First Amendment an *absolute prohibition* on Congress to take away certain rights," it is "hardly conceivable" that the Framers would, in

---

[32] Prudential Ins. Co. v. Cheek, 259 U.S. 530, 538 (1922).

[33] 268 U.S. 652, 666 (1925) (emphasis added).

[34] Levy, supra note 3 at 73. See Bator, supra text accompanying note 31.

[35] 268 U.S. at 672 (emphasis added). "Holmes was against extending the Fourteenth Amendment, Brandeis reported. But that meant, Brandeis said, that 'you are going to cut down freedom through striking down regulation of property, but not give protection [to freedom in other contexts]'." Alexander Bickel, *The Supreme Court and the Idea of Progress* 27 (1978) (brackets in the original).

the Fifth, provide that *"Congress might take away* the same rights by due process of law."[36]

When the First Amendment was proposed, Madison urged that "it was equally necessary that [free speech] be secured against the State governments," but his plea was fruitless.[37] Jefferson, the great champion of free speech and free press, wrote in 1804 to Abigail Adams, "While we deny that Congress have a right to controul the freedom of the press, we have ever asserted the right of the States, and their exclusive right to do so."[38] This was the premise on which the First Congress had acted in drafting the Bill of Rights. One may agree with Justice Benjamin Cardozo that free speech "is the matrix, the indispensable condition, of nearly every other freedom,"[39] but the fact remains that the one time the American people had an opportunity to express themselves on the issue in the First Congress, they rejected the application of the First Amendment to the States.

Charles Warren had prophesied in 1926 that by enlarging the Fourteenth Amendment to protect free speech, the Court had opened the door to adoption of the rest of the Bill of Rights.[40] Faced with mounting pressure to do so, Justice Cardozo, in *Palko v. Connecticut,*[41] fashioned a confining doctrine—"ordered liberty": some "immunities[42]

[36] Charles Warren, "The New 'Liberty' Under the Fourteenth Amendment," 38 Harv. L. Rev. 431, 441 (1925) (emphasis in the original).

[37] 1 *Annals of Congress* 435, 755 (1st Cong., 1st Sess., Gales & Seaton 1834; print bearing running head "History of Congress"). Supra text accompanying notes 4–6.

[38] Quoted in Felix Frankfurter, "John Marshall and the Judicial Function," 69 Harv. L. Rev. 217, 226 (1955).

[39] Palko v. Connecticut, 302 U.S. 319, 327 (1937).

[40] Warren, supra note 36 at 458–60.

[41] 302 U.S. 319 (1937).

[42] Jusice Cardozo confusingly referred to "the privileges and immunities that have been taken from earlier articles of the Federal Bill of

that are valid as against the federal government by force of the specific pledges of particular amendments have been found to be implicit in the concept of ordered liberty, and thus, through the Fourteenth Amendment, become valid as against the States." Such portions of the Bill of Rights as had been "absorbed" in the Amendment, he continued, rested on "the belief that neither liberty nor justice would exist if they were sacrificed." "Absorption" proceeded from those "principle[s] of justice so rooted in the tradition and conscience of our people as to be ranked as fundamental."[43] Plainly this was judicial rewriting of the Constitution in the teeth of the Founder's rejection of application of the Bill of Rights to the States. And it finds no warrant in the history of the Fourteenth Amendment, which associated "fundamental rights" with the "limited category" set out in the Civil Rights Act.

Insofar as "selective incorporation" derives from the due process clause, the argument runs into the evidence found by Dean James Bond in his study of the Ratification debates

---

Rights and brought within the Fourteenth Amendment by a process of absorption." 302 U.S. at 326–327. "Privileges and immunities" are located in Article IV (2), not in the Bill of Rights. Cardozo's mistaken reference led Curtis to conclude, "Prior to the adoption of the fourteenth amendment these privileges and immunities had been held to limit the power of the federal government only and not the states. So one could reasonably conclude from the *plain language* of the amendment that it was intended to extend the protection of the Bill of Rights against the states." Curtis, "Reply" 48 (emphasis added). Article IV (2), however, entitles a migrant from one State to the privileges and immunities of a citizen in another State, infra Chapter 7 text accompanying notes 12–20, and it has no application to the federal government. Nor can one obviously derive from the Amendment's "privileges or immunities of a citizen of the United States" an intention "to extend" the Bill of Rights "against the States." This exhibits both Curtis' misunderstanding of historical fact and his tendency to mistake assertion for proof.

[43] 302 U.S. at 325.

that "those who debated §1 of the 14th amendment paid scant attention to the due process clause."[44] The Republicans, he found, represented that "the due process clause guaranteed only procedural fairness."[45] Rarely was its meaning "elaborated." Any elaboration compared it to the Due Process Clause of the Fifth Amendment, and as Bond observes, "A phrase said to mean only what it meant in the fifth amendment could scarcely have been intended as a shorthand expression of every other right included in the Bill of Rights."[46] He concluded that "no one in these states [Illinois, Ohio, and Pennsylvania] believed that the due process clause protected any substantive rights, much less all those rights enumerated in the Bill of Rights. No one even hinted that the due process clause incorporated any—much less all—of the Bill of Rights guarantees."[47]

"Ordered liberty," wrote Louis Lusky, who is a friend to broad judicial power, "is a vehicle for whatever meaning the Court gives it, and thus enables the Court to apply its own conceptions of public policy."[48] Louis Henkin observed, "It

[44] James E. Bond, "The Original Understanding of the Fourteenth Amendment in Illinois, Ohio and Pennsylvania," 18 Akron L. Rev. 435, 461 (1985).

[45] Id. 443. The "usual meaning at that time was unquestionably procedural"; the "procedural rights of the accused in court, as well as the right to own property, to contract, to appear as witnesses, were what they principally had in mind." Joseph James, *The Framing of the Fourteenth Amendment* 198 (1965).

[46] Bond 457–58; see also Justice Frankfurter, infra chapter 7 text accompanying note 5.

[47] Bond 464.

[48] L. Lusky, *By What Right?* 105 (1975). He comments, "it is too vague to describe a national objective. It says that order and liberty are both to be sought, but provides no standard for reconciling the eternal conflict between them." Id. 107. Levy noted Frankfurter's view that "selective incorporation" provides "no formula other than 'a merely subjective test' for determining which rights were in and which were out." Levy, supra note 3 at 65.

is hardly possible to see" in the due process clause "some purpose to select some specifics of the Bill of Rights" and not the whole. "Ordered liberty," he justly considers, is an "uncertain, debatable, changeable touchstone," and it therefore lends itself to unlimited judicial manipulation.[49] Of Cardozo's touchstone, "the conscience of mankind," Henkin remarks, "there is no relation—historical, linguistic or logical—between that standard and the specific provisions, or any specific provision, of the Bill of Rights." It reduces to how "the Court reads that conscience,"[50] a most unreliable guide.

Several Justices have shared such views. In a book written by Justice Owen Roberts after his retirement, he stated in a passage quoted by Justice William Douglas, that the cases will fall "on one side of the line or the other as a majority of nine Justices appraise conduct as either implicit in the concept of ordered liberty or as lying without the confines of that vague concept."[51] Justice Byron White likewise re-

[49] L. Henkin, "Selective Incorporation in the Fourteenth Amendment," 73 Yale L.J. 78, 79 (1963).

Curtis urges that "After 'brooding over the matter,' Professor Fairman 'slowly' concluded, however, that 'implicit in the concept of ordered liberty' was about as close as one could come to the 'vague aspirations' that the framers had for the [privileges or immunities] clause." Curtis, Book 6. Like Curtis, who now "diverges from Crosskey in some significant ways," id. 8, I too may be permitted to differ with Fairman in this particular. To my mind the framers were quite clear as to the contents of the "privileges or immunities" clause; to them the clause did not represent "vague aspirations." Nor can the framers, deeply committed to States' rights, be charged with encroaching on the State sovereignty secured by the Tenth Amendment under cover of "vague aspirations."

[50] Id. 78, 75. Curtis considers that Palko reached "the right result for the wrong reason," Curtis, "*Reply*" 49. He pins his faith to the legislative history.

[51] O. Roberts, *The Court and the Constitution* 80 (1951), quoted in Poe v. Ullman, 367 U.S. 518–19 (1961), Douglas, J., dissenting. "Of course," Roberts added, "in this view, the due process clause of the Fifth Amend-

garded the concept as no more than a means whereby a majority of the Court can impose "its own philosophical predilections upon States legislatures or Congress."[52] And Justice Black maintained that the concept merely embodied "natural law due process notion[s] by which this Court frees itself from the limits of a written Constitution."[53] Cardozo's reliance on the "traditions and conscience of our people" is refuted by the refusal of the First Congress to apply the Bill of Rights to the States. That, to borrow from Learned Hand, was the "last formal expression" of the people's will.[54] No departure from that expression can be found in the history of the Fourteenth Amendment; instead, but for the narrow enclave of the Civil Rights Act, the framers clearly withheld from the Court power to intrude into State regulation of domestic affairs.

It needs constantly to be borne in mind that, as Judge Richard Posner reminds us, "apply the Bill of Rights to the

---

ment . . . may be repetitious of many of the other guarantees of the first eight amendments and may render many of their provisions superfluous," a result that argues against the "absorption" doctrine. Such considerations are brushed aside by Leonard Levy: the framers of the Bill of Rights "were in many respects careless, even haphazard, draftsmen. They enumerated particular rights associated with due process and then added the due process clause itself, probably as a rhetorical flourish, a reinforced guaranty, and a genuflection toward traditional usage." Levy, supra note 3 at 66. Chief Justice Taney, however, stated, "Every word appears to have been weighed with the utmost deliberation, and its force and effect to have been fully understood." Holmes v. Jennison, 39 U.S. (14 Pet.) 540, 571 (1840). For examples of the Framers' fastidious care in selecting words, see Raoul Berger, *Federalism: The Founders' Design* 92–93 (1987). Many Framers and Ratifiers sat in the First Congress and profited from Resolutions of the several States which accompanied the several Ratifications.

[52] Dissenting in Robinson v. California, 370 U.S. 660, 689 (1962).

[53] Dissenting in *In re* Winship, 397 U.S. 358, 381–82 (1970).

[54] Learned Hand, *The Spirit of Liberty* 14 (1952). The judge "has no right to divination of public opinion which runs counter to its last formal expression."

States through the due process clause and you weaken the states tremendously by handing over control of large areas of public policy to federal judges. . . . It is hard to believe that this was intended by all the state legislators whose votes were necessary to ratify the [fourteenth] amendment."[55] In a broader context, Horace Flack, a pioneer student of the Fourteenth Amendment, wrote that the Radical proposals were designed to "increase the powers of the Federal Government very much, but to do it in such a way that the people would not understand the great change intended to be wrought in the fundamental law of the land." He observed that "had the people been informed of what was intended by the Amendment [as envisaged by the Radicals], they would have rejected it."[56] They could not ratify what had not been disclosed.

Justice Samuel Miller, a contemporary of the Fourteenth Amendment and a keen observer of the political scene, declared shortly after adoption of the Fourteenth and Fifteenth Amendments,

> we do not see in those amendments any purpose to destroy the main features of the general system. Under the pressure of all the excited feeling growing out of the war, our statesmen have still believed that the existence of the states with power for domestic and local government . . . was essential to the working of our complex system of government.

And he rejected a construction that would subject States "to the control of Congress, in the exercise of powers heretofore universally conceded to them" in the absence of "language which expresses such a purpose too clearly to admit of doubt."[57] Chief Justice William Rehnquist considers that

[55] R. Posner, *The Federal Courts: Crisis and Reform* 194, 195 (1985). See also infra Chapter 4 text accompanying notes 10–15.

[56] Horace Flack, *The Adoption of the Fourteenth Amendment* 237 (1908).

[57] Slaughter-House Cases, 83 U.S. (16 Wall.) 36, 82, 78 (1872).

Miller was "one of the great justices";[58] and Harold Hyman, a Reconstruction historian, wrote of Miller's opinion in the *Slaughter-House Cases* that "the law world of the 1870s acquiesced . . . generally and tenaciously to Slaughter-House doctrine on federalism."[59] That view constitutes a contemporary construction that "on settled principles carries great weight."[60]

Hereafter I shall show that the Radical designs were defeated and that the Amendment was presented to the people as having very narrow scope, applicable to the South, not the North. Let it here suffice that David Donald, a Reconstruction historian, wrote, "Disturbed by the revolutionary changes Sumner hoped to bring about in the South, Republican Congressmen were horrified that he proposed to extend them to the North as well."[61] And Alexander Bickel noted that "Conservative Republicans who considered the Freedmen's Bill [applicable only in the South] an appropriate concession to offer to the Radicals evidently felt quite differently about a statute which might be applied to their constituencies."[62]

[58] W. H. Rehnquist, *The Supreme Court: How It Was, How It Is* 185 (1987).

[59] H. Hyman, "Federalism: Legal Fiction and Historical Artifact?" 1987 Brigham Young Law Review 905, 922.

[60] Justice William Johnson referred in 1827 to the presumption that the contemporaries of the Constitution have claims to our deference "because they had the best opportunity of informing themselves of the understanding of the framers of the Constitution, and of the sense put upon it by the people when it was adopted by them." Ogden v. Saunders, 25 U.S. (12 Wheat.) 212, 290 (1827).

[61] David Donald, *Charles Sumner and the Rights of Man* 299 (1970).

[62] A. Bickel, "The Original Understanding and the Segregation Decision," 69 Harv. L. Rev. 1, 40 (1955).

CHAPTER TWO

Antecedents of the Fourteenth Amendment

ONE who would understand the Fourteenth Amendment must begin with its relation to the Civil Rights Act of 1866, which proceeded on a parallel track in the Thirty-ninth Congress.[1] The framers considered that the Amendment was essential either to preserve the Act from repeal by a subsequent Congress or to constitutionalize it because of doubts concerning Congress' power to enact it.[2] On either theory, the Amendment did not go beyond the Act; the Act was deemed to be "incorporated" in the Amendment.

Preliminarily, two controversies generated by the Thirteenth Amendment need to be noted: (1) did it authorize enactment of the Civil Rights Act which shielded specified rights from discrimination; and (2) did it confer citizenship? First, in contrast to the Democrats, Michael Curtis asserts, "Republicans relied on the Thirteenth Amendment" for "power to pass the Civil Rights Act."[3] In fact, Republican opinion was divided.[4] John Bingham, among others, "was convinced" that Congress lacked power to pass the Act, a belief that Curtis considers was "probably correct."[5] At best,

[1] Curtis, Book 57.
[2] For citations see Berger, *Judiciary* 23 note 12.
[3] Curtis, Book 81.
[4] Supra note 2.
[5] Curtis, Book 107, 103. United States v. Harris, 106 U.S. 629, 643 (1882),

there was a conflict of opinion.[6] Harold Hyman, an activist sympathizer, acknowledged that there was "a large stream of constitutionalism [for the] argument that the thirteenth amendment diminished state's powers not one whit beyond abolition."[7] Hyman's statement is at war with Curtis' assertion that "only a handful of Republicans . . . thought Congress lacked power to pass the Civil Rights Bill."[8]

Second, although the slaves had been emancipated, the *Dred Scott* decision cast a shadow over their citizenship. Hence, the freedmen were made "citizens of the United States" by the Civil Rights Bill because, Senator Lyman Trumbull explained, he wished "to end the very controversy, whether the negro was a citizen or not."[9] Late in consideration of the Fourteenth Amendment it was proposed to make one born in the United States a citizen thereof and of the State wherein he resided. Senator Jacob Howard stated that "this settles the great question of citizenship and removes all doubts as to what persons are or are not citizens of the United States."[10] So too, Justice Miller referred to *Dred Scott* and said, "To remove this difficulty primarily . . . the first section was framed. . . . That its main purpose was

---

rejected the notion that "under a provision of the Constitution which simply abolished slavery and involuntary servitude, we should with few exceptions, invest Congress with power of the whole catalog of crimes."

[6] Supra note 2.

[7] H. Hyman, *A More Perfect Union* 428 (1973).

[8] Curtis, Book 80. Of a disagreement between Wilson and Bingham about whether Congress had power to enact the Civil Rights Bill under other constitutional provisions, Curtis remarked, "To remove such doubts was one of the reasons the Fourteenth Amendment was passed." Curtis, Book 126.

[9] Globe, 39th Cong., 1st Sess. 1285 (1866). Curtis states, "According to Trumbull, blacks were made citizens by the Thirteenth Amendment." Curtis, Book 49. Candor calls for recognition that "according to Trumbull" the issue was controverted.

[10] Globe 2890.

to establish the citizenship of the negro can admit of no doubt."[11] Patently, the Thirteenth Amendment sheds little, if any, light on the meaning of the Fourteenth.

THE CIVIL RIGHTS ACT

The Civil Rights Act did not stop with the bestowal of citizenship but went on to specify certain rights that were to be free of discrimination, testimony that the rights did not, in the framers' view, flow automatically from the bestowal of citizenship.[12] Before examining the Bill it needs to be stressed that the framers deemed the Bill and the Fourteenth Amendment to be *identical*. A grasp of the scope of the Bill therefore will inform us as to the ambit of the Amendment. As Fairman stated, "over and over in this debate [on the Amendment] the correspondence between Section One of the Amendment and the Civil Rights Act is noted. The provisions of the one are treated as though they were essentially identical with those of the other."[13] Thus, George Latham stated that "the 'civil rights bill' which is now a law . . . covers exactly the same ground as the amendment."[14] Martin Thayer said, "[I]t is but incorporating in the Constitution the principle of the civil rights bill which has lately become a law."[15] Howard Jay Graham, an early advocate of an abolitionist reading of the Amendment, stated that "virtually every speech in the debates on the amendment—Republican and Democrat alike—said or agreed that the Amendment was designed to embody or in-

---

[11] Slaughter-House Cases, 83 U.S. (16 Wall.) 36, 73 (1872).
[12] See Shellabarger, infra Chapter 6 text accompanying note 19.
[13] Fairman, 44.
[14] Globe 2833.
[15] Avins 213.

corporate the Civil Rights Act."[16] Horace Flack, a broad constructionist of the Amendment, wrote, "[N]early all said that it was but an incorporation of the Civil Rights Bill. . . . there was no controversy as to its purpose or meaning."[17] In a contemporaneous decision, Justice Bradley declared that "the first section of the bill covers the same ground as the Fourteenth Amendment."[18]

The Civil Rights Act was a response to the Black Codes whereby the South sought to set emancipation at naught.[19] Senator Henry Wilson said that "the vagrant laws of [Virginia] were used to make slaves of men whom we have declared to be free."[20] The codes "set up elaborate systems of bound apprenticeship, labor restrictions, vagrancy laws, limits on property ownership and craft employment," virtually chaining a black to his habitat.[21] Trumbull tellingly de-

[16] H. J. Graham, *Everyman's Constitution* 391, note 73 (1968).

[17] H. Flack, *The Adoption of the Fourteenth Amendment* 81 (1908). For similar expressions during the Ratification campaign, see infra Chapter 4 text accompanying notes 20–22.

[18] Livestock Dealers' & Butchers' Ass'n v. Crescent City Live-Stock Landing Co., 15 F. Cas. 649, 655 (C.C.D. La. 1870) (No. 8, 408).

[19] The "major inspiration for the 1866 law," Alfred Kelly wrote, "was the resentment and alarm that the enactment of the 'Black Codes' . . . had produced among the Radical Republicans." A. Kelly, "Clio and the Court: An Illicit Love Affair," 1965 S. Ct. Rev. 119, 147. The Joint Committee on Reconstruction noted the "acts of cruelty, oppression and murder, which the local authorities are at no pains to prevent or punish." Avins 94.

[20] Avins 138. "The bald declaration by Edmund Rhett of South Carolina—'the general interest both of the white men and of the negroes requires that he should be kept as near to the condition of slavery as possible' . . . sums up the purpose of the Black Codes." Morton Keller, *Affairs of State* 202–4 (1977).

[21] Keller, supra note 20 at 203. For additional citations see Berger, *Judiciary* 24–25; and see the ordinance of Opalusas, La., Avins 130. Curtis observes that "The codes restricted such basic rights as the freedom to move, to contract, to own property, to assemble, and to bear arms. . . . Republicans were unwilling to tolerate such deprivations, as the passage

scribes some of these Black Codes. That "of Mississippi provides that no negro shall own or hire lands . . . that he shall
not sue or testify against a white man; that he must be employed by a master before the second Monday in January or
he will be bound out—in other words sold into slavery."
The Code of Alabama provides that "if a negro who has
contracted to labor . . . runs away he shall be punished as a
vagrant." What that meant is illustrated by the Tennessee
Code: "the vagrant negro may be sold to the highest bidder
to pay his jail fees."[22]

Senator William Stewart explained that the Civil Rights
Bill was designed "simply to remove the disabilities existing by laws tending to reduce the negro to a system of
peonage. It strikes at that; *nothing else.* . . . That is the
whole scope of the law."[23] Earlier, Senator Henry Wilson
had urged the framers to ensure that the freedman "can go
where he pleases, work when and for whom he pleases; that
he can sue and be sued; that he can lease and buy and sell his
own property, real and personal."[24] The "one pervading
purpose" of the Fourteenth Amendment, said Justice Samuel Miller, "was the protection of the newly-made freeman
and citizen from the oppression of those who formerly exercised unlimited dominion over him."[25] That clearly had no
application to the North.

Section 1 of the Bill squarely took aim at these evils,
providing in pertinent part,

---

of the Civil Rights Bill would show." Curtis, Book 35. The Bill made no
provision for a right to "assemble or bear arms" nor did any spokesman
for it read these terms into the bill.

[22] Avins 135.

[23] Id. 204 (emphasis added).

[24] Id. 98.

[25] Slaughter-House Cases, 83 U.S. (16 Wall.) 36, 71, 81 (1872). Senator
Timothy Howe, "a pronounced radical," 6 Charles Fairman, *History of the*

> That there shall be no discrimination in civil rights or immu-
> nities . . . on account of race . . . but the inhabitants of every
> race . . . shall have the same right to make and enforce con-
> tracts, to sue, be parties and give evidence, to inherit, purchase,
> lease, sell, hold and convey real and personal property, and to
> full and equal benefit of all laws and proceedings for the secu-
> rity of person and property, and shall be subject to like punish-
> ments . . . and to none other.[26]

This specific enumeration reflected a sentiment expressed at
the outset by Senator John Sherman, who desired to secure
such rights to the freedmen, "naming them, *defining precisely* what they should be."[27] The words "civil rights and
immunities" had aroused concern, for Martin Thayer explained that "to avoid any misapprehension" as to what the
"fundamental rights of citizens" are, "they are stated in the
bill. The same section goes on to define with greater particularity the civil rights and immunities which are to be
protected by the bill." "[T]hat enumeration," he added,
"precludes any possibility that the general words which
have been used can be extended beyond the particulars
which have been enumerated."[28]

Despite such assurances, Bingham, draftsman of the Fourteenth Amendment, took violent exception to the "oppressive" scope of the Bill:

Supreme Court of the United States 1297 (1971), emphasized that the South
denied "the plainest and most necessary rights of citizenship. The right to
hold land . . . the right to collect their wages by the processes of law . . .
the right to appear in the courts, as suitors for every wrong done them."
Globe, S. App. 219. See infra Chapter 4 text accompanying notes 7–14.

[26] Avins 121.

[27] Id. 97 (emphasis added).

[28] Id. 169. Against such particularization Bingham's reference "to the
Civil Rights bill as a bill providing for enforcement of the Bill of Rights,"
Curtis, Book 72, carries little weight, the less because he was neither man-
ager nor leading spokesman on behalf of the Bill.

[T]he term "civil rights" as used in this bill does include and embrace *every* right that pertains to the citizen as such. . . . If civil rights has this extent, what, then, is proposed by the provision of the first section? Simply to strike down by congressional enactment every State constitution which makes a discrimination on account of race or color in *any* of the civil rights of the citizen. . . . By the constitution of my own State [Ohio] neither the right of the elective franchise nor the franchise of office can be conferred [except] upon a white citizen. . . . Now what does this bill propose? To *reform the whole criminal and civil Code* of every State government.[29]

Justice Black, for whom Bingham was an authoritative expositor, observed that Bingham objected to the Civil Rights Bill because "it would actually strip the states of the power to govern, centralizing all power in the Federal government. To this he was opposed."[30] Bingham's expostulation led to the deletion of "civil rights and immunities." James Wilson, chairman of the House Committee on the Judiciary and manager of the bill for the House, explained that in order to remove

the difficulty growing out of any other construction *beyond the specific rights named* in the section, our amendment strikes out all of those general terms and leaves the bill with the rights specified in the section.

The deletion was made, he said, because

some gentlemen were apprehensive that the words we propose

[29] Avins 186, 188 (emphasis added). The phrase there shall be no discrimination in civil rights "must be stricken out," Bingham said, "or the constitutions of the States are to be abolished." Id. at 186.

Hamilton had assured the 1787 Ratifiers that "There is one transcendent advantage belonging to the province of the State governments . . . the ordinary administration of criminal and civil justice." Federalist No. 17 at 103 (Mod. Lib. ed. 1937).

[30] Adamson v. California, 332 U.S. 46, 100 (1947) (dissenting opinion).

to strike out might give warrant for a *latitudinarian construction not intended.*[31]

The effect of the Bingham-Wilson incident was summarized by the Supreme Court in *Georgia v. Rachel* (1966):

> The legislative history of the 1866 Act clearly indicates that Congress *intended to protect a limited category* of rights. . . . [T]he Senate bill did contain a general provision forbidding "discrimination in civil rights or immunities" preceding the specific enumeration of rights. . . . Objections were raised in the legislative debates to the breadth of the rights of racial equality that might be encompassed by a prohibition so general. . . . [A]n amendment was accepted striking the phrase from the bill.[32]

Coming after many Republican statements of unorthodox "beliefs,"[33] this incident cries out for explanation. How can the bar to a "latitudinarian construction," the emphasis on the named "specific rights," be reconciled with an effort to read the Bill of Rights into the Bill? Why did Bingham, who so strenuously protested against an "oppressive" invasion of the States' domain, embrace in the lesser "privileges" of the Amendment the very purpose he had rejected in the Bill? Opposed to those earlier unorthodox "beliefs" is the undeniable fact that the House voted for the deletion, that the "oppressive" language is missing from the Act.[34] The fact is, as Alexander Bickel observed, the words "no discrimination in Civil Rights" had been deleted because Republicans "who had expressed fears concerning its reach . . . would have to go forth and stand on the platform of the

---

[31] Avins 191 (emphasis added).

[32] 384 U.S. 780, 791 (1966) (emphasis added).

[33] Infra, Chapter 7 test accompanying notes 46–59, and infra text accompanying notes 40–48.

[34] Act of April 19, 1866, 14 Stat. 27.

fourteenth amendment."[35] They simply dared not hold out to the Ratifiers that the North, which had not been guilty of the offensive practices of the South, would be deprived of control over its own civil and criminal administration.

But we must not expect logical progression from Bingham. Notwithstanding his ringing condemnation of the "oppressive" scope of the Bill's "civil rights," of its purported reform of "the whole civil and criminal code of every State," he yet proposed in the very same speech to enforce the Bill of Rights against the States,[36] unaware that he would thus in great part accomplish the very outreach that he had condemned. Earlier he had explained, after quoting from *Barron v. Baltimore,* that

> although *as ruled* the existing amendments *are not applicable to and do not bind the States,* they are nevertheless *to be enforced* and observed in the States by the grand utterance of that immortal man, who while he lived, stood alone in intellectual power among the living men of his country, and now that he is dead, sleeps alone in his honored tomb by the sounding sea—Daniel Webster.[37]

Intoxicated by his own rhetoric, Bingham does not pause to inquire on what theory are laws that "do not bind" to be "enforced."[38] Are we to conclude that the practiced lawyers who listened to Bingham would exalt a Webster utterance above a Marshall decision that remained the reigning law,[39]

[35] A. Bickel, "The Original Understanding and the Segregation Decision," 69 Harv. L. Rev. 1, 61–62 (1955).

[36] Avins 186; see supra note 29 and infra text accompanying note 37.

[37] Avins 158.

[38] "Bingham is one who used ringing rhetoric as a substitute for rational analysis." Wallace Mendelson, "Mr. Justice Black's Fourteenth Amendment," 53 Minn. L. Rev. 711, 716 (1969).

[39] See infra Chapter 5 text accompanying note 94. The lawyers on the Joint Committee substituted precise legal concepts for Bingham's impressionistic verbiage. His draft referred to the "equal protection" clause

putting to one side the irrelevancy of the Webster quotation? Stevens, leader of the Radicals, said the Fourteenth Amendment was needed because "the Constitution limits only the action of Congress, and is not a limitation on the States."[40] Certainly, Bingham's colleagues in the Joint Committee did not accept every word that fell from his lips as gospel. According to Benjamin Kendrick, editor of the Committee's Journal, Bingham "stood almost alone. . . . a great many Republicans, including the entire New York delegation, were opposed to [his proposed] amendment."[41] Curtis notes that "Despite Bingham's appeal, many were not convinced."[42] Not long after, Stevens, also a member of the Committee, stated, "In all this contest about reconstruction I do not propose either to take his counsel, recognize his authority, or believe a word he says."[43] It is more reasonable to conclude that the Framers acted on Bingham's representation that he drew for "privileges or immunities" on Article IV (2),[44] whereunder the words had acquired an accepted connotation.

In truth, Bingham's confusion and hairpin turns could only confuse his hearers. Consider his emphasis in the "oppressive" speech on the reserved rights of the States: "The Constitution does not delegate to the United States the

---

of the Fifth Amendment, from which it was notably absent. The lawyers substituted its due process clause and a separate equal protection provision. Curtis, Book 62. So too, he at first employed the Article IV terms— "the citizens in each State"—which would have left the situation unchanged. See Avins 158. Presumably the lawyers perceived the need to shift to "citizen of the United States."

[40] Curtis, Book 86.
[41] Benjamin Kendrick, *The Journal of the Joint Committee on Reconstruction* 214–15 (1914); Flack 59.
[42] Curtis, Book 71.
[43] Cong. Globe 39th Cong., 2d Sess. 816 (Jan. 28, 1867).
[44] Curtis, Book 63; Avins 150.

power to punish offenses against the life, liberty, or property of the citizen in the States . . . but leaves it as the reserved power of the States, to be by them exercised."[45] Again, "the care of the property, the liberty, and the life of the citizen, under the solemn sanction of an oath imposed by your Federal Constitution, is in the States, and not in the Federal Government. I have sought to effect no change in that respect in the Constitution of the country."[46] So too, "I have always believed that the protection in time of peace within the States of *all* the rights of person and citizen was of the powers reserved to the States. And so I still believe. . . . Now what does this [Civil Rights] bill propose? To reform the whole civil and criminal code of every State government."[47] What sense did it make to inveigh against a "reform of the whole civil and criminal code of every State" and in the same breath insist that the criminal and civil provisions of the Bill of Rights must be enforced against the States? This goes beyond a charge of inconsistency; it suggests that Bingham's confused utterances must have confused his listeners.[48] Moreover, they *voted* to delete a threat "to reform" the States' civil and criminal codes, and it offends common sense to conclude that they veered with Bingham and accepted an "unorthodox" theory that the Bill of Rights governed their codes. Then too, James Wilson assured the House that "we are not making a general criminal code for the States."[49]

[45] Avins 186.
[46] Id. 187.
[47] Id. 188.
[48] See also infra Chapter 9 text accompanying notes 10–13, 15–17.
[49] Avins 165.

CHAPTER THREE

"Privileges or Immunities"

WITH Justice Harlan, I agree that the "privileges or immunities" clause was "expected to be the primary source of substantive protection; the Equal Protection and Due Process Clauses were relegated to a secondary role, as the debates and other contemporary materials make clear."[1] Nevertheless, in the *Slaughter-House Cases* (1872) the Supreme Court virtually deprived the clause of meaning,[2] and in the more than one hundred years that have since elapsed, that judgment has been left standing. Since the ongoing debate in large part pivots on the meaning of the clause, it will be instructive to seek historical light on what it meant to the framers.

The terms "privileges and immunities" are first met in Article IV of the Articles of Confederation:

> The better to secure and perpetuate mutual friendship and intercourse among the people of the different states in this union, the free inhabitants of each of these states . . . shall be entitled to all privileges and immunities of free citizens in the several states; and the people of each state shall have *free ingress and*

[1] Oregon v. Mitchell, 400 U.S. 112, 164 (1970). In his study of the Ratification debates, Dean Bond found that the "debate focussed primarily on the privileges and immunities clause." Bond 445.

[2] 83 U.S. (16 Wall.) 36 (1872). The "effect of the decision was to make the privileges and immunities clause practically a dead letter." Stanley Morrison, "Does the Fourteenth Amendment Incorporate the Bill of Rights?" 2 Stan. L. Rev. 140, 144 (1949).

regress to and from any other state, and shall enjoy therein all the *privileges of trade and commerce* . . . as the inhabitants thereof respectively.[3]

For the Founders the enumerated "privileges of trade and commerce" limited the general words "privileges and immunities."[4]

Conforming to their drive for compressed utterance, the Framers phrased Article IV (2) more succinctly:

The citizens of each State shall be entitled to all Privileges and Immunities of Citizens in the several States.

There was no discussion of this provision in the Federal Convention, suggesting familiarity with its terminology, the more because a large number of delegates, Madison included, had been members of the Continental Congress and were familiar with the Articles of Confederation.

Contemporary with adoption of the Fourteenth Amendment, the Court in *Paul v. Virginia* spoke of Article IV (2) in terms of the antecedent Articles of Confederation provision: "it gives them the right of free ingress into other States and regress from them," a tacit identification of the two articles.[5] Shortly thereafter, Justice Miller stated in the *Slaughter-House Cases:*

---

[3] H. S. Commager, *Documents of American History* III (7th ed. 1963) (emphasis added).

[4] Madison stated in Federalist No. 41 at 269 (Mod. Lib. ed. 1937): "For what purpose could the enumeration of particular powers be inserted, if these and all others were meant to be included in the preceding general power? Nothing is more natural or common than first to use a general phrase, and then to explain and qualify it by a recital of particulars. But the idea of an enumeration of particulars which neither explain nor qualify the general meaning . . . is an absurdity." Cited by Joseph Story, *Commentaries on the Constitution of the United States* §911 at 664 (5th ed. 1905).

[5] 75 U.S. (8 Wall.) 168, 180 (1968).

There can be but little question that the purposes of both these provisions is the same, and that the privileges and immunities intended are the same in each. In the Articles of Confederation we have some of these specifically mentioned, and perhaps enough to give some general idea of the class of civil rights meant by the phrase.[6]

Fifty years later Chief Justice White declared in *United States v. Wheeler* that "the text of article IV §2 of the Constitution makes manifest that it was drawn with reference to the corresponding clause of the Articles of Confederation and was *intended to perpetuate its limitations*."[7] The limited scope of Article IV (2) delineated by these cases was confirmed even earlier—before the Fourteenth Amendment—by other cases.

In the first of these cases, *Campbell v. Morris* (1797), Justice Samuel Chase, soon to become a Justice of the Supreme Court, stated on behalf of the Maryland Court that counsel were agreed

> that a particular and *limited operation* is to be given these words [privileges and immunities] and not a full and comprehensive one. . . . The court are of the opinion it means . . . the peculiar advantages of acquiring and holding real as well as personal property, that such property shall be protected and secured by the laws of the state, in the same manner as the property of the citizens of the state is protected.[8]

In explaining the Civil Rights Bill, Senator Lyman Trumbull, chairman of the Senate Judiciary Committee, read a more extended version of these remarks to the Senate.[9] An-

[6] 83 U.S. (16 Wall.) 36, 75 (1872).

[7] 254 U.S. 281, 294 (1920) (emphasis added). Curtis notes the relation of Article IV (2) to the pedecessor Article IV of the Articles of Confederation. Curtis, Book 65.

[8] 3 H. & McH. 535, 554 (Md. 1797).

[9] Avins 121.

other opinion, *Abbott v. Bayley,* was rendered by the Massachusetts Court in 1827, stating in part,

> The privileges and immunities secured to the people of each State in every other State can be applied only in case of removal from one State to another. . . . They shall have the privileges and immunities of citizens; that is they . . . may take and hold real estate; and may, according to the laws of such State, eventually enjoy the full rights of citizenship without the necessity of being naturalized.[10]

This too was read by Trumbull to the Senate.[11]

Then Trumbull read from *Corfield v. Coryell,* an opinion by Justice Bushrod Washington on circuit (1823),[12] saying that "he enumerates the *very rights* belonging to a citizen of the United States which are *set forth in the first section* of this bill."[13] For the convenience of the reader an extended quotation is here set out:

> The next question is, whether this act infringes that section of the Constitution [Article IV (2)] which declares that "the citizens of each State shall be entitled to all privileges and immunities of citizens in the several States"? The inquiry is, what are the privileges and immunities of citizens in the several States? We feel no hesitation in *confining these expressions* to those privileges and immunities which are *in their nature fundamental,* which belong of right to the citizens of all free governments; and which have at all times been enjoyed by the citizens of the several States which compose this Union, from the time of their becoming free, independent and sovereign. What *these fundamental principles* are it would perhaps be more tedious than difficult to enumerate. They may, however, be *all comprehended* under the following general heads: protection by the

[10] 6 Pick. 89, 91 (Mass. 1827).
[11] Avins 121.
[12] 6 F. Cas. 546 (C.C.E.D. Pa. 1823) (No. 3220) (emphasis added).
[13] Avins 122 (emphasis added).

Government; the enjoyment of life and liberty, with the right to acquire and possess property of every kind; and to pursue and obtain happiness and safety, subject, nevertheless to such restraints as the Government may justly prescribe for the general good of the whole. The right of a citizen of one State to pass through, or to reside in any other State, for purposes of trade, agriculture, professional pursuits, or otherwise; to claim the benefit of the writ of *habeas corpus;* to institute and maintain actions of any kind in the courts of the State; to take, hold, and dispose of property, either real or personal, and an exemption from higher taxes or impositions than are paid by other citizens of the State, may be mentioned as some of the *particular privileges* and immunities of citizens which are clearly embraced by the general description of privileges *deemed fundamental;* to which may be added the elective franchise, as regulated and established by the laws or constitutions of the States in which it is to be exercised.[14]

Trumbull immediately pointed out that the Bill did not provide for the elective franchise.[15] The exclusion of suffrage alone argues against an expansive reading of *Corfield.* Senator Sumner regarded suffrage as *"the only sufficient guarantee,"* later adding that if the Fourteenth Amendment "is inadequate to protect persons in their . . . right to vote, it is inadequate to protect them in anything."[16]

Reliance on *Corfield* for an expansive interpretation is misplaced, if only because Washington went on to say, "[W]e cannot accede to the proposition . . . that, under this provision [Article IV (2)] of the Constitution the citizens of the several States are permitted to participate in *all* the rights

---

[14] This was read to the Senate by Trumbull, id. (emphasis added).

[15] Id.

[16] Globe 685 (emphasis in the original); Cong. Globe, 40th Cong., 3d Sess. 1008 (1869). Without suffrage, said Senator Samuel Pomeroy, the Negro "has no security." Globe 1182.

which belong exclusively to the citizens of any other particular State."[17] It denied an out-of-state migrant the right
to dredge for oysters in New Jersey waters, hardly evidenc-
ing an expansive interpretation. Curtis translates *Corfield* as
"recognizing Article IV as protecting a set of basic national
liberties," relying on Justice Roberts in *Hague v. C.I.O.*:
"the purpose of this section was to create rights of citizens
of the United States. . . . Such was the view of Justice
Washington."[18] *Corfield* furnishes no evidence for that view.
Instead, after reciting the Article IV provision, which refers
to "the citizens *of each State*," it said "The inquiry is, what
are the privileges and immunities of citizens *in the several
States*," not of the United States, later referring to the "right
of *a citizen of one State* to pass through, or to reside, in any
other." An erroneous reading is not legitimized because it
comes from the Court. Be it assumed that *Corfield* is more
comprehensive than the rights the Civil Rights Act enumerates, it yet may not be invoked to enlarge the scope of the
later Act. Trumbull hastened to disclaim *Corfield's* inclusion
of suffrage and underscored the "very rights . . . which are
set forth in the first section." We should not substitute *Corfield* for the Act's own and later enumeration.

[17] Curtis, Book 67. Corfield held that a migrant could not dredge for
oysters in the host State.
   [18] Id.

CHAPTER FOUR

The Ratification Debate

AFTER canvassing the Ratification materials, Charles Fairman concluded that they confirm that the Bill of Rights was not incorporated in the Amendment.[1] That view is powerfully buttressed by Dean James Bond's recent study of the Ratification debates in Illinois, Ohio, and Pennsylvania.[2] It contains striking repetitions of the views expressed by the Framers.

The vast bulk of the Ratification sources are newspaper articles and reports of campaign speeches. With the exception of Pennsylvania, Dean James Bond states, the State legislatures kept no records of their debates. The legislative debate in Pennsylvania, he comments, "reads like a reprise of the six month campaign debate that preceded it."[3] There are a few Governor's messages, but "most are quite general."[4] In the three States on which Bond concentrated, he observes that debate "did not focus exclusively or even primarily on the first section of the 14th amendment. The principal issue in those states was control of the national government."[5] Republicans feared that Democrats would wrest control of the House because with emancipation Southern

---

[1] Fairman 81 et seq.
[2] Bond 435. See also Curtis, Book 145.
[3] Bond 461.
[4] Curtis, Book 145.
[5] Bond 438.

representation would no longer be limited to three-fifths of the blacks as Article I (3) provided. Now each voteless freedman counted as a whole person, a threat that section 2 of the Fourteenth Amendment countered by making representation proportional to enfranchisement of the blacks.[6]

Let us for the moment retrace our steps. "Disturbed by the revolutionary change Sumner hoped to bring about in the South," wrote Senator Sumner's biographer, David Donald, "Republican Congressmen were horrified that he proposed to extend them to the North as well."[7] Those who cite violations of free speech *in the South,* denials of protection *in the South*[8] where freedmen were terrorized, maimed, and murdered,[9] overlook that the North was given little or no reason to conclude that it too was the target of the Amendment. In fact, remarks made by leading spokesmen in the Thirty-ninth Congress would lead the framers to believe that the Civil Rights Bill would have no operation in the North. James Wilson said that "If the States would all practice the constitutional declaration [of Article IV (2)] . . . and enforce it . . . we might very well refrain from the enactment of this bill into a law."[10] Northern States respected the rights secured by Article IV (2). Senator Trumbull likewise had stated that the Bill "will have no operation where . . . all persons have the same civil rights without regard to color or race."[11] The Civil Rights Bill, said Senator

[6] Berger, *Judiciary* 15–16.

[7] David Donald, *Charles Sumner and the Rights of Man* 299 (1970).

[8] Curtis, Book 134, 135, 138, 144, 147, 148.

[9] Bond 449, 444; supra Chapter 2 note 19; infra Chapter 6 text accompanying note 51; see Chapter 8 text accompanying note 11.

[10] Avins 163–64. James Wilson said that blacks "must have the same liberty of speech in any part of the South as they have always had in the North." Curtis, Book 144.

[11] Avins 122. In his criticism of President Johnson's veto of the Civil Rights Bill, Senator Trumbull said, "This bill in no manner interferes

Stewart, was designed to forestall "reduc[ing] the negro to a system of peonage." If all the Southern States will repeal such laws, he continued, this Bill "will simply be a nullity"; it will have "no operation." [12]

Such expressions strikingly surface in the Ratification debates. Joseph James, who independently sifted the Ratification materials, concluded that

> Wherever the framers discussed the amendment, it was presented as a necessary limitation to be placed on the South to safeguard the Union. Though the possibility of its operation to some extent in the North had been pointed out in Congress[?], such statements formed no part of the Republican campaign procedure.[13]

Proponents of the Amendment, wrote Bond, "downplayed the extent to which Congress would interfere with State authority." [14] It is inconceivable, given attachment to State sovereignty over local matters,[15] that the North would tamely have accepted drastic curtailment of its own control of criminal administration.

It will be recalled, as Bond also notes, that the Civil Rights

---

with the municipal regulations of any State which protects all alike in their rights of person and property. It would have no operation in Massachusetts, New York, Illinois or most of the States in the Union." Avins 200.

[12] Id. 204.

[13] James 167. On August 31, 1866, Columbus Delano "pointed out that the first section [Fourteenth Amendment] was made necessary by the perilous position of Northern men and loyal Southerners in the South." Id. 162. James noted that on July 18, 1866, Governor Norton of Indiana said that the reason for the due process clause provision "was the discrimination practiced by the Southern States." Id. 159. See also Senator Howe, supra Chapter 2 note 25. And James states that "The possibility of [the amendment's] operation in the North was seldom alluded to and often denied." Id. 191.

[14] Bond 458.

[15] Chapter 5 text accompanying notes 22–45.

Bill had been fueled by the Black Codes, which "convinced" the Republican majority that "white Southerners intended to reinstitute slavery by denying newly freed blacks the rights to contract, to hold property and sue,"[16] precisely the particularized rights enumerated in the Bill. This was the "limited category" of rights which the framers considered were "identical" with and incorporated in the Amendment. Speaking in Chicago in August 1866, Senator Trumbull, who had piloted the Bill through the Senate, "clearly and unhesitatingly declared §1 of the Amendment to be 'a re-iteration of the rights as set forth in the Civil Rights Bill,'"[17] which did not include any reference to the Bill of Rights. In Indiana, Senator Lane "affirmed Trumbull's statement concerning the first section"; and Senator Sherman "endorsed" those views in a speech on September 29, 1866.[18] Senator Poland spoke to the same effect in November 1866.[19]

In sum, "statements of congressmen before their constituents definitely identify the provisions of the first section of the amendment with those of the Civil Rights Bill."[20] The "simple, most commonplace explanation of the first section," Bond wrote, was that "it constitutionalized the Civil Rights Bill." He concluded that the "citizen's under-

[16] Bond 443.
[17] James 161.
[18] Id. 162, 164.
[19] Curtis, Book 252 note 46. In Pennsylvania, "proponents explained over and over again that §1 wove the principles of the Civil Rights Bill into the Constitution. Senator Bingham bluntly stated that §1 embodied the Civil Rights Bill. . . . Representative Day cheerfully admitted that the purpose of §1 was 'to write in substance the civil rights bill'." Bond 461–62.

When the amendment was submitted to the States for ratification, states Horace Flack, "the northern press with few exceptions, if any, took the view that the first section of the Amendment re-enacted or gave authority for the Civil Rights Bill." Flack 145.
[20] James 179.

standing of §1 of the 14th amendment" was that "it simply 'made constitutional' the Bill's guarantee of civil rights."[21] This identification is confirmed by the repeated emphasis that the "indispensable" civil rights were "the right to contract, to sue, to testify, and otherwise resort to the courts; to hold and transfer property; and to the full and equal benefit of all laws for the protection of person and property."[22]

When a stump speaker expanded on the point, "he generally listed the very rights enumerated in the Civil Rights Bill . . . the right to sue . . . to be protected in their person and property, the right of locomotion—the right to go where they please and . . . own property where they please."[23] Curtis downgrades this evidence: "*Several* congressmen" made "these *vague* statements."[24] But he acknowledges that a speech by Senator John Sherman saying that "the sum and substance of the first clause was the right to come and go, to sue, and to make contracts," "seems inconsistent with incorporation of the Bill of Rights."[25] He admits, in other words, what I have steadily maintained, that the enumeration of particular rights in the Civil Rights Bill excludes the unmentioned Bill of Rights. When proponents of the amendment "explained that §1 protected civil rights or civil liberty," Bond concluded, "they could scarcely have had in mind a different set of civil rights from those they had so shortly before included in the Civil Rights Bill."[26]

In sum, Dean Bond has shown that the Ratification debates confirm the legislative history with respect to the view

[21] Bond 443, 448.
[22] Id. 446, 447.
[23] Id. 448
[24] Curtis, Book 141, 253 note 46 (emphasis added).
[25] Id. 253 note 46 (emphasis added).
[26] Bond 448–49.

that the Civil Rights Act and the Fourteenth Amendment were "identical," that the Amendment, like the Act, aimed to protect the rights to contract, hold property, and have access to the courts, and have the rights of locomotion— "liberty" as defined by Blackstone, and that the Act was designed to operate in the South.

PART II

Opposition Views

CHAPTER FIVE

Some Preliminary Considerations

SO convincing, in my judgment, is the evidence hereinbefore set forth that, to borrow the words of van Alstyne, it is indeed "astonishing that the answer should be thought doubtful at this late date."[1] Nevertheless, he hails Michael Curtis' recent challenge to the established learning[2] as the "most powerful response to doubts respecting the incorporation doctrine yet published."[3] He is joined by Leonard Levy, who considers that "Curtis alters the path of scholarship with his excellent work."[4] Eugene Gressman also weighs in, stating that Curtis "does a masterful job in undermining the Berger-Fairman thesis and in demonstrating the faulty and short-sighted nature of their examination of the framers' 'original intention'."[5] Notwithstanding their august imprimatur, it will appear, as Curtis said of Fair-

[1] Supra Chapter 1 text accompanying note 2.

[2] Id. note 2.

[3] Id. "Foreword" at ix. Van Alstyne is not an unbiased observer. Earlier he had dismissed my views out of hand as "narrow." W. van Alstyne, "Interpreting the Constitution: The Unhelpful Contributions of Special Theories of Judicial Review," 35 U. Fla. L. Rev. 209, 234 note 65 (1983). For the reason why, see Berger, *Judiciary* 69–76, 419–27.

[4] Levy, dust jacket of the Curtis book. In 1972, Levy concluded that "the historical record is inconclusive." L. Levy *Judgments: Essays in American Constitutional History* 136 (1972).

[5] E. Gressman, "Book Review," 1 New Law Books Reviewer 57, 59 (1986).

man, that "much of [Curtis's] mountain of evidence is beside the point."[6]

To proponents of judicial activism, Curtis' book is understandably welcome, for it seems to supply historical justification, draped in all the trappings of scholarship, for their activist advocacy. It is of the genre described by a fellow activist, Paul Brest, as "not political theory but advocacy scholarship—amicus briefs ultimately designed to persuade the Court to adopt our various notions of the public good."[7] Curtis was moved to write because he is alarmed that "A rollback of civil liberty is well underway" because "Berger's analysis may give impetus to a reaction already begun," that "would strip citizens of federal protection against state infringement of their rights to freedom of speech."[8] Gressman observed that Curtis has "a passionate concern for civil liberties,"[9] thereby exhibiting his commitment to a thesis. "Motivation," Curtis has written, "is not important if the

[6] Curtis, Book 100. All is grist that comes to Curtis' mill. Consider, "Senator Trumbull submitted a petition from citizens of Quincy, Illinois, demanding absolute equality of political as well as civil rights," id. 56, in light of Trumbull's explanation that political rights were excluded from the Civil Rights Bill, supra Chapter 3 text accompanying note 15. In the event, suffrage was left to the States by the Fourteenth Amendment. Berger, *Judiciary* 52–68. See also infra Chapter 8 note 77 (Senator Howard). For the anti-Negro sentiment in southern Illinois, see infra, Chapter 6 text accompanying notes 88 and 89.

[7] P. Brest, "The Fundamental Rights Controversy: The Essential Contradiction of Normative Scholarship," 90 Yale L.J. 1063, 1109 (1981). Levy wrote, "History for the activist is a protean instrument, useful for legitimating a predetermined result." Levy, supra note 4 at 78.

[8] Curtis, *Reply* 47, 46.

[9] Gressman, supra note 5 at 57. Gressman himself is not dispassionate; he brands the *Slaughter-House* decision as "infamous," id. at 60, that is, of "shameful badness, vileness, or abominableness." *Oxford Universal Dictionary* (1955). As a contemporaneous construction, *Slaughter-House* is scarcely deserving of such utter reprobation. See supra Chapter 1 text accompanying notes 58–59.

facts are true."[10] Passionate dedication to a cause, however, is apt to distort the judgment of what the facts are, to promote wishful thinking, and to result in partisan propaganda. As John Morley observed, "passion appears hopelessly fatal to anything like success in the pursuit of truth, who does not reveal herself to followers thus inflamed."[11] Curtis' partisanship leads him to fall short of scholarly duties. For example, one who undertakes to tear down the scholarship of others is under a duty of unimpeachable accuracy, of stating their position fairly,[12] duties he does not perform.

Curtis' thesis did not spring from the blue. He tells us that "most influential on [his] thought" was the "powerful critique" of Fairman's article by William Crosskey, which

[10] Michael Curtis, "Judge Hand's History: An Analysis of History and Method in *Jaffree v. Board of School Commissioners of Mobile County*," 86 W. Va. L. Rev. 109, III (1983).

[11] F. N. Hirst, *Early Life and Letters of John Morley* 94 (1927). As long ago as 1942, I indicated that I liked it no better when Justice Black read my predilections into the Constitution than when the Four Horsemen read in theirs. Raoul Berger, "Constructive Contempt: A Post-Mortem," 9 U. Chi. L. Rev. 602 (1942). Thus I am opposed to antiabortionists, to prayer in the schools, and yet consider that the respective Supreme Court decisions in those cases are without constitutional warrant. Morley lauded the "temper which seeks truth for its own sake apart from the consequences, and apart from its agreement or disagreement with reigning convictions." Hirst, supra at 96.

[12] Curtis cannot bring himself to state his opponent's case fairly and accurately. For example, "Berger's analysis contains contradictions. First *he* said that Bingham's references to the Bill of Rights meant and were understood to mean only the due process clause of the Fifth Amendment and article IV, section 2." Curtis, Book 123. He cites (page 249, note 240) to page 141 of my *Judiciary* where it states, "As *Fairman* pointed out, the antecedent of [Bingham's] remark was Article IV sec. 2, and the Fifth Amendment due process clause which Bingham equated with equal protection." So it was not Berger but Fairman who "said." Moreover, Bingham himself stated, as Curtis noted (Book 57), that "The Congress shall have power to make all laws which shall be necessary and proper to se-

"brilliantly illuminates the forgotten relation of the Fourteenth Amendment to the Bill of Rights,"[13] taking no notice of Fairman's devastating reply.[14] It is an eloquent comment on the weight of Crosskey's article that Justice Black, writing fourteen years after the article appeared, as Curtis notices, "unfortunately did not cite Crosskey."[15] Black, who clung to his theory despite the Court's obdurate rejections, would have been eager to embrace some solid historical confirmation. His omission to cite Crosskey's impassioned elaboration of his theory testifies that Black had little confidence in Crosskey's scholarship. Crosskey, it must be stated bluntly, was an untrustworthy scholar.[16] One example must suffice. Despite the legislative history confirmation that the Bill of Rights was not to apply to the States, Crosskey dismissed Marshall's "iniquitous doctrine of *Barron v. Baltimore*" as "*without any warrant at all.*"[17] But as Dean John Hart Ely recently wrote, "in terms of the original under-

---

cure to citizens of each state all privileges and immunities of citizens in the several states (Art. IV, Sec. 2); and to all persons in the several states equal protection in the rights of life, liberty, and property (Fifth Amendment)." Throughout, Curtis reduces incontrovertible facts to Berger's bare assertions.

[13] Curtis, Book 121, 8.

[14] Charles Fairman, "A Reply to Professor Crosskey," 22 U. Chi. L. Rev. 144 (1954).

[15] Curtis, *Reply* 49 note 22.

[16] For more extended documentation, see Raoul Berger, *Congress v. The Supreme Court* 22–46 (1969).

[17] William Crosskey, *Politics and the Constitution in the History of the United States* 1076, 1091 (1953). Julius Goebel wrote that "Crosskey's performance, measured even by the least exacting of scholarly standards, is . . . without merit . . . Mr. Crosskey . . . coming to his task with a new axe to grind has seemingly forsworn all canons of objectivity to make himself a grindstone that suits his purposes." J. Goebel, "Book Review," 54 Colum. L. Rev. 450, 451 (1954). "History," Levy observes, "was on the side of the Supreme Court." Levy, *supra* note 4 at 67.

standing, *Barron* was almost certainly decided correctly."[18]
The soundness of *Barron* has been, and remains, virtually
beyond dispute, regardless of the Fourteenth Amendment.
That said, I agree with Sidney Hook that "What makes a
thing true is not who says it, but the evidence for it."[19] Consequently, I shall painstakingly examine the "facts" Curtis
musters in his effort to overthrow conventional learning.

It is a splendid irony that a judicial activist such as Curtis
should rely on the "original intention" of the framers,[20] a
doctrine that is anathema to his fellow activists and which
they have consigned to outermost limbo.[21] But they cannot
have it both ways; selective application of original intention
according to whether it serves a particular purpose is obviously arbitrary. Then too, in seeking to ascertain the original intention, I have ever confined myself to an intention
that is *clearly* discernible. Curtis' "history," as will appear, is
rarely clear and very often conflicting, and therefore is an
inconclusive index of the original intention.

GUIDES TO INTERPRETATION

A. *State Sovereignty*

For understanding the scope of the Fourteenth Amendment, the continued attachment of the North to State control of internal affairs is far more important than the
abolitionist antislavery background upon which Curtis so
heavily relies. Tarnished as State sovereignty was by the in-

---

[18] J. H. Ely, *Democracy and Distrust* 196 (1980).

[19] Sidney Hook, *Philosophy and Public Policy* 121 (1980).

[20] Curtis, Book 9–12.

[21] Levy, who extols Curtis, wrote that issues of public policy "should
not be decided merely because of the original meaning of words in the
Constitution," and derides "an antiquarian historicism that would freeze
[the Constitution's] original meaning." Levy, *supra* note 4 at 71.

iquities of slavery for which it was invoked by the South, the North remained deeply attached to the principle of States' Rights. Although the North was determined to bar the return of the emancipated slaves to serfdom by the South's Black Codes,[22] eradication of inequality, as C. Vann Woodward remarked, would require "a revolution in the North as well"[23]—a revolution for which the North was unprepared,[24] and, as we have seen, of which it was not really apprised. The "radical leaders," Horace Flack wrote, "were as aware as any one of the attachment of a great majority of the people to the doctrine of States Rights . . . the right of the States to regulate their own internal affairs."[25] At the outset, Roscoe Conkling, a member of the Joint Committee on Reconstruction, said, "the proposition to prohibit States from denying civil or political rights to any class of persons, encounters a great objection on the threshold. It trenches upon the principle of existing local sovereignty."[26] Other Republicans were of the same mind.[27] John Bingham, draftsman of the Fourteenth Amendment, also recognized that "the citizens must rely upon the State for their protection. I admit that such is the rule under the Constitution as it now stands." And thereupon he read to his fellows Madison's statement in Federalist No. 45:

[22] "The Black Codes had convinced a majority in Congress that white Southerners intended to reinstitute slavery by denying newly freed blacks the rights to contract, hold property and sue." Bond 443. See also supra Chapter 2 text accompanying notes 42–47.

[23] C. V. Woodward, *The Burden of Southern History* 79 (1960).

[24] Supra Chapter 4 text accompanying notes 8–14.

[25] Flack 68. H. J. Graham, *Everyman's Constitution* 312 (1968): "No one reading the debates carefully will question the framers' devotion to federalism, even the extreme radicals."

[26] Avins III.

[27] For example, Robert Hale said, "all powers having reference to the relationship of the individual to the municipal government, the powers

The power reserved to the Federal States will extend to all the objects which, in the ordinary course of affairs concerns the lives, liberties, and properties of the people, and the internal order, improvement, and prosperity of the State.[28]

Like his Ohio colleague Bingham, Columbus Delano said, "[T]here are certain rights of citizenship that are exclusively within the control of the States."[29] And George Latham stated that Congress "has no right under the Constitution to interfere with the internal policy of the several States."[30] Such sentiments were summarized by a sagacious observer, Justice Samuel Miller, shortly after adoption of the Fourteenth Amendment:

> We do not see in these amendments any purpose to destroy the main features of the general system. Under the pressure of all the excited feeling growing out of the war, our statesmen have still believed that the existence of the States with powers for domestic and local government . . . was essential to the perfect working of our complex form of government.[31]

As Don Fehrenbacher has recently concluded, there was a "widespread and tenacious resistance to the interventionism federalism aggressively embodied."[32]

---

of local jurisdiction and legislation, are in general reserved to the States." Id. 153. See also George Latham, id. 190–91; Columbus Delano, id. 178.

[28] Avins 159. Madison also stated in No. 39 of the Federalist that the jurisdiction of the proposed federal government "extends to enumerated objects only, and leaves to the States a residuary and inviolable sovereignty over all other objects." Federalist No. 39 at 249 (Mod. Lib. ed. 1937).

Bingham repeated, "the care of the property, the liberty, and the life of the citizen . . . is in the States and not in the Federal Government. I have sought to effect no change in that respect." Avins 187.

[29] Avins 178.

[30] Id. 190–91.

[31] Slaughter-House Cases, 83 U.S. (16 Wall.) 36, 82 (1872).

[32] Don E. Fehrenbacher, *The Dred Scott Case: Its Significance in American Law and Politics* 581 (1978).

It is against this tide of historical evidence that Curtis asserts, "[L]eading Republicans gave the states' rights argument short shrift,"[33] citing William Lawrence, who said, [I]t is better to invade the judicial power of the State than to permit it to invade, strike down, and destroy the civil rights of citizens."[34] Lawrence directed his fire at Southern restrictions on the freedmen. Outraged by the Black Codes, the North set out to protect a set of fundamental rights that would enable emancipated slaves to exist.[35] But the North was far from ready to clothe the former slaves with a full panoply of rights, the less because it was apprehensive of undue interference with the States' right to order their own internal affairs.[36] Thus, Senator James Patterson of New Hampshire was "opposed to any law discriminating against [blacks] in the security and protection of life, liberty, person and property," but said that "beyond this I am not prepared to go."[37] For him, "life, liberty, and property" did not have

[33] Curtis, Book 118.

[34] Id.

[35] As Lawrence stated, "It is idle to say that a citizen shall have the right to life, yet to deny him the right to labor whereby alone he can live. It is a mockery to say that a citizen may have a right to live, and yet deny him the right to make a contract to secure the privileges and the rewards of labor." Avins 206. See also supra Chapter 2 text accompanying notes 19–25.

[36] Michael Perry, himself an activist, concurs in the view that the "proposition that the Fourteenth Amendment incorporates the Bill of Rights constitutes an invasion of rights reserved to the States by the Tenth Amendment, an invasion of such magnitude as to demand proof that such was the framers' intention." M. Perry, "Book Review," 78 Colum. L. Rev. 685, 690 (1978). The point was made by Judge Richard Posner, supra Chapter 1 text accompanying note 55.

[37] Globe 2699. See also Senator Stewart, infra text accompanying note 52. Curtis stresses that the "most common Republican refrain in the thirty-ninth Congress was that the life, liberty, and property of American citizens must be protected against denial by the States." Curtis, Book 41. But he acknowledges that "Although Republicans rejected the notion that states could invade the fundamental rights of citizens, they wanted to

the unbounded compass that Curtis throughout his book assigns to those terms. Delano, concerned lest blacks could serve as jurors, believed that citizens' rights "are to be guaranteed by the laws of the States . . . and by Congress . . . when there is power given by the Constitution . . . to enforce those rights." But he did "not believe that the rights of the States are utterly overwhelmed and dethroned."[38] And Bingham, as we have seen, made an even more forcible objection.[39] This "commitment to traditional state-federal relations meant," Alfred Kelly wrote, that "the radical Negro reform program could be only a very limited one."[40]

---

preserve the states. They did not want the federal government to supplant them altogether or usurp their basic functions." Id. Given that no Black Codes threatened black rights in the North, it is incumbent on Curtis to prove that the North knowingly consented to federal usurpation of State control over criminal and civil administration. Moreover, the framers, as will appear, associated "fundamental" rights with the limited category enumerated in the Civil Rights Bill. See also supra Chapter 4 text accompanying notes 8–14.

[38] Avins 178. It is difficult to reconcile this statement with Curtis' attribution to Delano of "associat[ing] individual liberties with Bill of Rights liberties." Curtis, Book 41.

Judge Robert Hale, a New York Republican, warned the House that "there are other liberties as important as the liberties of the individual citizen, and those are liberties and rights of the States." Avins 155. Senator Oliver Morton, an Indiana Republican, stated in 1868, "I still recognize the doctrine of States rights. There are rights that belong to the States, secured by the same Constitution that secures the rights of this Government, and therefore they are equally sacred." Avins 324. In the House, John Farnsworth of Illinois, who had been a proponent of the Fourteenth Amendment, said in 1871, "I do not believe in centralization of the power of Government, nor in abolishing the State lines or State governments or abridging their powers." Avins 508.

[39] Supra Chapter 2 text accompanying notes 29–32.

[40] A. Kelly, "Comment on Harold H. Hyman's Paper" in *New Frontiers of American Reconstruction* 55 (H. Hyman ed. 1966). Hyman notes Republican unwillingness "to travel any road more rugged than the Civil Rights-Freedman's Bureau extension—fourteenth amendment route that left the

Given this deeply rooted devotion to preservation of State control over internal matters, underscored by the Tenth Amendment,[41] equivocal or confused utterances must not be construed to curtail State sovereignty. One who argues for such curtailment has the burden of proof.[42] Writing in 1954, Herbert Wechsler observed that there is "a burden of persuasion on those favoring national intervention" in State matters.[43] The exceptional nature of federal intervention was underscored in 1938 by Justice Louis Brandeis. The Constitution, he wrote, "preserves the autonomy and independence of the States"; federal supervision of their action "is in no case permissible *except* as to matters specifically delegated to the United States. Any interference . . . *except* as thus permitted is an invasion of the authority of the State."[44]

states master of their own fates." H. Hyman, *A More Perfect Union* 470 (1973); see also id. 440, 448. The pervasive attachment to federalism-State control of local institutions, Phillip Paludan repeatedly emphasizes, was "the most potent institutional obstacle to the Negroes' hope for protected liberty." P. Paludan, *A Covenant With Death* 15, 31, 51, 54 (1975).

[41] Senator Frederick Frelinghuysen, who read the Fourteenth Amendment broadly, agreed in 1871 that

The fourteenth amendment must . . . not be used to make the General Government imperial. It must be read . . . together with the tenth amendment. . . . Thus reading the fourteenth amendment . . . I do not consider it now expedient for the General Government to assume a general municipal jurisdiction over crime in the States.

Avins 542.

[42] Raoul Berger, *Federalism: The Founders' Design* 151–57 (1987).

[43] H. Wechsler, "The Political Safeguards of Federalism: The Role of the States in the Composition and Selection of the National Government," 54 Colum. L. Rev. 543, 545 (1954).

[44] Erie Ry. Co. v. Tompkins, 304 U.S. 64, 78–79 (1938) (emphasis added). The undelegated, "residuary and inviolable" powers (Federalist No. 39 at 249), expressly guaranteed by the Tenth Amendment, are not to be curtailed under cover of what Chief Justice Rehnquist referred to as the "vaguely worded prohibitions against state action," the "fuzzy gener-

Earlier, in the *Slaughter-House Cases*, Justice Miller had rejected a construction of the Fourteenth Amendment that would subject States "to the control of Congress in the exercise of powers heretofore universally conceded to them" in the absence of "language which expresses such a purpose too clearly to admit of doubt."[45] These were but expressions of the principle earlier formulated by Chief Justice Marshall: an "opinion which is . . . to establish a principle never before recognized should be expressed in plain and explicit terms."[46] Curtis' inferences from his collation of Republican statements fails to take this rule of construction into account.

B. *Abolitionism vs. Racism*

Curtis labors under the grand illusion that the Fourteenth Amendment was "produced" by "the anti-slavery crusade."[47] He notes that "Prior to the Civil War prejudice against blacks was extensive." While only "a handful of radical political abolitionists" had advocated the abolition of slavery before Lincoln espoused its cause, he asserts that "radical abolitionism had become Republican orthodoxy by 1866" as a "result of Lincoln's support for emancipation."[48] So he is led to conclude that the far-reaching program of some abo-

---

alities" of the Fourteenth Amendment. W. H. Rehnquist, *The Supreme Court: How It Was, How It Is* 180 (1987).

In Noble State Bank v. Haskell, 219 U.S. 104, 110 (1911), the Court itself stated, per Justice Holmes, that "as it often is difficult to mark the line where what is called the police power of the states is limited by the Constitution of the United States, judges should be slow to read into the latter a *nolemus mutare* as against the law-making power."

[45] 83 U.S. (16 Wall.) 36, 78 (1872).

[46] United States v. Burr, 25 F. Cas. 55, 165 (C. C. Va. 1807) (No. 14,693). For an extreme application of this rule, see Pierson v. Ray, 386 U.S. 547, 554–55 (1967).

[47] Curtis, Book 6.

[48] Id. 29, 34.

litionists equally commended itself to most Republicans. Triumphantly he asks, "If abolitionists' ideas were an anathema to most Republican Congressmen, why in the previous session of Congress had they abolished slavery in the states— the main goal of the radical political abolitionists?"[49] It escapes him that, unfortunately, a northerner could oppose slavery and yet remain a racist. The matter was cogently summarized by Henry Monaghan:

> We forget that many mid-nineteenth century Americans, perhaps a clear majority, opposed slavery and racial equality with equal intensity. They could logically believe that emancipation required that the freed man possess certain rights to personal security and property. Simultaneously they could favor rank discrimination against blacks in political and social matters.[50]

The fact, noted by David Donald, is that racism "ran deep in the North," and the suggestion that "Negroes should be treated as equals to white men woke some of the deepest and ugliest fears in the American mind."[51] While Senator William Stewart considered that Negro suffrage "will endanger our national existence," he said, "I am not in favor of turning the negro over to oppression in the South. I am in favor of legislation . . . that shall secure him a chance to live, a chance to hold property, a chance to be heard in the courts."[52]

The framers of the Fourteenth Amendment represented a constituency that had just emerged from a wrenching, bitterly fought war, a war that left them drained physically and emotionally. It had begun with a drive to save the Union

---

[49] Id. 118.

[50] H. Monaghan, "The Constitution Goes to Harvard," 13 Harv. C.R. & C.L. Rev. 117, 126 (1978).

[51] D. Donald, *Charles Sumner and the Rights of Man* 202, 252 (1970).

[52] Avins 106.

and had gone on to emancipate the slaves. Now the war-weary North was far from ready to embark on fresh crusades for the realization of still other abolitionist goals. The North was finally converted to abolition of slavery not so much by abolitionist theorizing—abolitionists were widely disliked if not hated[53]—but because slavery had led to a bloodbath.[54] That "peculiar institution" had to be destroyed. But it by no means follows that the North swallowed abolitionist theorizing whole.

Abolition of slavery, it needs to be remembered, did not touch the North, for there slavery did not exist. Bingham asked, "Is the bill of rights to stand in our Constitution hereafter as in the past five years within eleven [Southern] States, a mere dead letter?,"[55] recognition that the mischief did not extend to the North. Curtis himself observes that "Republican congressmen *typically* insisted on protection . . . within the Southern states."[56] "Whereas the Thirteenth Amendment," which abolished slavery, Fairman noted, "had been generally popular among Northerners, the Civil Rights Bill, as James G. Blaine recalled, was legislation 'of a different type', which, particularly in the Middle and Western States,

[53] The "abolitionists were regarded throughout most Northern Circles as disagreeable and intemperate radicals and were heckled, harrowed, and even killed by Northern mobs." Dan Lacy, *The White Use of Blacks in America* 54 (1972); see also Curtis, Book 39. For the persistence of such feelings, see infra text accompanying notes 80–90.

[54] James Russell Lowell wrote, "our war has not been distinctly and avowedly for the extinction of slavery, but a war rather for the preservation of our national power and greatness, in which the emancipation of the negro was forced upon us by circumstances and accepted as a necessity." J. R. Lowell, "Abraham Lincoln," in 28 Harvard Classics 441, 455 (1910).

[55] Avins 158.

[56] Curtis, Book 56 (emphasis added); see supra Chapter 4 text accompanying notes 7–15.

touched upon deep feelings."[57] Obliviousness to such facts leads Curtis to assert, "The major fault with Professor Fairman's effort to understand the Fourteenth Amendment is that it overlooked the antislavery origins of the amendment."[58] But it is, in fact, Curtis who turns his back on the two powerful countervailing tides of public opinion during this period of our history—pervasive detestation of the abolitionists and rampant racism in the North.

Although Curtis recognizes that "Prior to the Civil War prejudice against blacks was extensive," he overlooks its continuing virulence during and after the War. It does not suffice to cite Lincoln's 1856 remark about equality in the Declaration of Independence[59] while ignoring his later re-

[57] 6 Charles Fairman, *History of the Supreme Court of the United States* 1168 (1971). Robert Hale of New York protested that Bingham's amendment "takes away from these States the right to determine for themselves what their institutions shall be. Oregon has not been contumacious towards this Union." Avins 155.

[58] Curtis, Book 100. Levy likewise wrote in 1972 that "the evidence of 1866–1868 [the framers' debates] must be read in the light of a received tradition of abolitionist constitutional argument." Levy, supra note 4 at 70.

[59] Curtis, Book 16–17. In 1789 "the democratic movement was in abeyance, and a 'thermidorian reaction' in full swing. . . . The Federal Constitution put a stopper on those levelling and confiscatory demands of democracy." S. E. Morison & H. S. Commager, *The Growth of the American Republic* 300 (1950). It is an historical fallacy to read modern mores back into the Declaration of Independence. Jefferson, who penned it, predicted emancipation, but wrote, "it is equally certain that the two races will never live in a state of equal freedom . . . so insurmountable are the barriers which nature, habit and opinion have established between them." Quoted in Alexis de Tocqueville, *Democracy in America* 378 (1900). In truth, the Constitution did not embody the "equality" sounded in the Declaration, as Stevens pointed out to the framers. Globe 536. On March 18, 1868, he reiterated, "The Constitution of 1787 did not carry out the principles of government which were intended by the fathers when in 1776 they laid the foundations. . . . the actions of the Convention in framing the Constitution . . . bartered away for the time being some of those inalienable rights." Cong. Globe, 40th Cong., 2d Sess. 1767 (1868).

marks to a delegation of black leaders who called on him in the White House:

> There is an unwillingness on the part of our people, harsh as it may be, for you free colored people to remain with us. . . . [E]ven when you cease to be slaves, you are far removed from being placed on an equality with the white man. . . . I cannot alter it if I would. It is a fact.[60]

Fear that emancipated slaves would flock north in droves and compete with white labor alarmed the North.[61] The letters and diaries of Union soldiers, C. Vann Woodward recounts, reveal an "enormous amount of antipathy towards Negroes."[62]

Racism, Reconstruction historian David Donald recounts, "ran deep in the North."[63] For this the debates in the Thirty-ninth Congress furnish abundant confirmation. George Julian, an Indiana Radical, deplored the "proverbial hatred" of Negroes; the "real trouble," he said, "is we hate the Negro." Senator Henry Lane referred to the almost "ineradicable prejudice"; Senator William Stewart spoke of the "nearly insurmountable prejudice"; and James Wilson re-

[60] Woodward, *supra* note 23 at 81.

[61] C. V. Woodward, "Seeds of the Failure in Radical Reconstruction Policy," in *New Frontiers of American Reconstruction* 121, 128, 131, 132 (H. Hyman ed. 1966). James Blair said that the working men of the North desire that the blacks who "are going North" should be "provided with a more suitable home than is to be found among the white population." Avins 36. In 1862, Senator Lyman Trumbull reprehended "a tirade against the State of Illinois because we do not want to receive the free negroes of Virginia." Id. Senator Thomas Hendricks of Indiana stated, "The policy of the State has been to discourage their immigration. . . . [T]he people have been unwilling that the white laborer shall be compelled to compete for employment with the negro." Avins 230.

[62] Woodward, supra note 23 at 82, 83. The "reaction of the average Union veteran to his contacts with the freedmen bordered on contempt." S. E. Morison, *The Oxford History of the American People* 715 (1965).

[63] Donald, supra note 51 at 202.

minded his fellows of the "iron-cased prejudice" against the blacks.[64] These were not foes of protection for blacks; rather they were Republican and Radical proponents of black protection. Notwithstanding, John Sherman stated in the Senate in 1867, "We do not like Negroes. We do not conceal our dislike."[65] As late as 1869, Henry Wilson, a Massachusetts Radical, could state in the Senate that "There is not today a square mile in the United States where the equal rights and privileges of those colored men has not been in the past and is not now unpopular."[66]

Consider Curtis' treatment of such facts: "*Berger asserted*" that these Congressmen "were influenced by 'Negrophobia'."[67] But even Curtis' own "authority," Harold Hyman, wrote, "Negrophobia tended to hold even the sparse Reconstruction institutions that the nation created to low throttle, and played a part in Reconstruction incompleteness."[68] The fact is, as Hyman's disciple Phillip Paludan noted, racism was "as pervasive during Reconstruction as after. Americans clung firmly to a belief in the basic inferiority of the Negro race, a belief supported by the preponderance of nineteenth-century scientific evidence."[69] "What lies beneath the politics of Reconstruction, so far as it touched the Negro," wrote Russell Nye, "is the prevailing racist policy tacitly accepted by both parties and the general public."[70]

All this is ironically dispatched by Curtis:

Still, they [the framers] were willing to invade state's rights, as conventionally understood, to protect blacks whom they *sup-*

---

[64] Globe 257, 739, 911, 2799, 2948.

[65] Woodward, supra note 61 at 128.

[66] Avins 340.

[67] Curtis, Book 118 (emphasis added).

[68] Hyman, supra note 40 at 447.

[69] Paludan, supra note 40 at 54.

[70] Russell Nye, "Comment on C. V. Woodward's Paper," in *New Frontiers of American Reconstruction* 148, 152 (1966).

posedly disliked. But they were not willing to interfere with states' rights by requiring the states to obey the Bill of Rights guaranties that protect whites and blacks alike.[71]

Like others who share his current sentiments, he refuses to see that the North's readiness to protect blacks from the South's attempt to reimpose the shackles of serfdom did not mean that the North was ready to surrender control of its own administration of other local, internal affairs.

There are similar problems in Curtis' account of abolitionist influence. He does not grasp that pre–Civil War abolitionist speeches during the drive to abolish slavery did not reflect postwar sentiment in the North. "Racism was a potent weapon for Democrats."[72] William Lloyd Garrison, the indomitable abolitionist who had been "dragg[ed] through the streets of Boston with a rope around his neck to be hanged,"[73] "accurately sensed the new mood when he declared that antislavery societies served no useful purpose now that slavery was abolished and closed down the *Liberator.*"[74] Curtis' emphasis on abolitionist influence on "antislavery activists," ignores the antiabolitionist feeling in the North and in the Thirty-ninth Congress. Woodward observed that during the war years, "The great majority of citizens in the North still abhorred any association with abolitionists,"[75] scarcely fertile soil for the sowing of abolitionist ideology. Senator William Fessenden, Cochairman of the Joint Committee on Reconstruction, similarly held the "extreme radicals" in "abhorrence."[76] Senator Edgar

[71] Curtis, Book 118 (emphasis added). See Monaghan, supra text accompanying note 50.

[72] Curtis, Book 29. See infra Chapter 6 text accompanying notes 87–88.

[73] Curtis, Book 39.

[74] Donald, supra note 51 at 233.

[75] Woodward, supra note 23 at 73.

[76] Benjamin Kendrick, *The Journal of the Joint Committee of Fifteen on Reconstruction* 257 (1914).

Cowan ridiculed the notion that the "antipathy that never sleeps, that never dies, that is inborn, down at the foundation of our natures," is "to be swept away by a half-dozen debates and the reading of half-a-dozen reports from certain abolitionist societies."[77] And Thaddeus Stevens—"The Scourge of the South"[78] was openly "hated" by many moderate Republicans.[79] In the Joint Committee, Stevens' "measures were more often voted against than voted for."[80] His Senate counterpart, Charles Sumner, was "distrust[ed]" when not "detested."[81] Senator Trumbull scathingly commented in 1870 that "it has been over the idiosyncrasies, over the unreasonable propositions, over the impractical measures" of Sumner "that freedom has been proclaimed and established."[82]

The nature of abolitionist theorizing, moreover, won little favor with the majority of framers of the Fourteenth Amendment. Curtis notices attempts by "antislavery lawyers" to develop "some remarkable theories" to "undergird their legal attack on slavery."[83] Joel Tiffany, a leading abolitionist theorist, for example, held that "slavery was unconstitutional, even in the states."[84] Some Republicans "believed that slavery in the territories . . . would deprive slaves of due process of law";[85] and John Bingham had argued that "the due process clause had banned slavery in federal territories." He thought that "slavery was incompatible

[77] Globe 343, 344—45.
[78] Fawn Brodie, *Thaddeus Stevens: The Scourge of the South* (1959).
[79] Id. 259.
[80] Id. 268.
[81] Donald, supra note 51 at 248.
[82] M. Benedict, *A Compromise of Principle* 39 (1974).
[83] Curtis, *Reply* 54; see Graham, infra text accompanying note 94.
[84] Curtis, Book 42.
[85] Id. 46.

with the Bill of Rights."[86] But the fact, as Curtis notes, is
that doctrines such as Tiffany's "were not accepted by most
Republican Congressmen."[87] Curtis recognizes that "in contrast to radical abolitionists, most Republicans admitted
that slaves were unprotected by the Constitution,"[88] and
that none of "the political platforms of the major antislavery
parties . . . advocated interference with slavery in the states
where it already existed."[89] Mainstream views were firmly
anchored in historical fact, to mention only Madison's assurance to the Virginia Ratifying Convention that "the Constitution did not allow interference with slavery in the States."[90]
This was not undone by the later due process clause; the
Fifth Amendment was not intended to nullify the carefully
framed compromises on the slavery issue. Nevertheless,
Curtis urges that "Tiffany's theories provided the basis for a
plausible civil libertarian reading of the Constitution."[91]

Even among abolitionists there were renowned dissenting voices—William Lloyd Garrison and Wendell Phillips
"rejected . . . radical antislavery constitutional thought."[92]
A neo-abolitionist, Howard Jay Graham who, Curtis considers, "contributed much to our understanding of the antislavery origins of the Fourteenth Amendment,"[93] wrote
that the abolitionist theory of racialized due process was

[86] Id. 47, 102. On the other hand, Bingham said that slaves "were not
protected by the Constitution." Id. 101, a contradiction not noticed by
Curtis.
[87] Id. 42.
[88] Id. 46. In his debates with Douglas, Lincoln said, "we have no right
to disturb slavery in the States where it exists." H. M. Hyndman, *Further
Reminiscences* 334 (1912).
[89] Curtis, Book 91.
[90] Id. 19.
[91] Id. 42–43.
[92] Id. 45.
[93] Id. III.

"rankly, frankly heretical."[94] The lawyers who sat in the
Thirty-ninth Congress were unlikely to embrace "rankly,
frankly heretical" views out of hand. Curtis' pervasive ana-
lytical flaw is his tacit assumption that the conservative-
moderate majority which, according to M. L. Benedict,
controlled the Thirty-ninth Congress, was converted by the
"rankly heretical" views of the abolitionists. That conversion runs counter to fact.

In truth, a Republican conservative coalition,[95] Benedict
has shown, "enacted their program with the sullen acquiescence of some radicals and over the open opposition of
many."[96] Benedict is in accord with David Donald.[97] And he

---

[94] Graham, supra note 25 at 242. "Some Republicans," Curtis notes,
"frankly recognized that their constitutional views were unorthodox."
Curtis, Book 52. Graham wrote,

> That this antislavery constitutional theory was extremely heterodox is
> clear. It was not primarily the product of minds trained in vigorous
> case analysis or statutory construction. It confused moral with civil
> and constitutional rights. It made the Declaration of Independence
> the basic constitutional document . . . the Federal Bill of Rights a
> *source* rather than a *limitation* of federal power."

Graham, supra notes 25 at 237–38.

[95] For example, Senator Trumbull, oft-quoted by Curtis, "was a Republican leader of preeminent influence. . . . Throughout Reconstruction as a whole he tended to be conservative." Curtis, Book 73.

[96] Benedict, supra note 82 at 210. Benedict's statement is rendered by
Curtis as "*Berger said* that a Republican centrist-conservative coalition
was in control of the Thirty-ninth Congress." Curtis, Book 118. To prove
the "attitude of congressional Republicans towards Reconstruction," he
cites Benedict for "there was much agreement among Republicans on
fundamentals." Id. 37. It is true that they were united in abolishing slavery, but Radical attempts to go much further were rejected. Benedict
concluded that the "radicals did not dominate Congress during the Reconstruction era. More Republicans (scaled consistently) conservative
than Radical"; in the House "consistent non-radicals (Conservative and
Centrists) still outnumbered radicals." Benedict, supra at 27, 23. Benedict
notes that "Senate Reconstruction policy after 1865 was framed by a non-

is confirmed by the defeat by a vote of 125 to 12 in the House and 34 to 4 in the Senate of radical insistence that Tennessee provide for Negro suffrage[98]—what Senator Sumner insisted was "the only sufficient guarantee" for black security.[99] This was after the submission of the Fourteenth Amendment to the Ratifiers. It is such votes, not what abolitionists had said outside the halls of Congress, that illuminate the framers' intent. Senator Sherman told a Cincinnati audience in September 1866, during the Ratification campaign, that "we defeated every radical proposition in it,"[100] an assurance meant to gratify his constituency.[101] Senator

---

radical Joint Committee on Reconstruction and a conservative Judiciary Committee." Id. 37. "Between them they fashioned the conservative Reconstruction program of the 39th Congress." Id. 146–47.

David Donald observed that "Moderates had to check extreme Radical proposals or be defeated in the districts they represented." D. Donald, *The Politics of Reconstruction* 51–52 (1965). For similar expressions during the Ratification campaign, see infra Chapter 6 text accompanying notes 66–71. See also Bickel, infra Conclusion note 6.

[97] Donald, supra note 96 at 51–52. Commending the Fourteenth Amendment, Senator Richard Yates said, "If we do not meet the views of the Radicals . . . we at all events have the medium, the moderation which has been agreed upon." Avins 237. Morton Keller stated, "It is true that the *specifics* of Reconstruction policy were determined primarily by moderate leaders such as Senator Lyman Trumbull and William Fessenden," who sought "to limit the degree to which the federal government interceded to protect the civil rights of the freedmen." M. Keller, *Affairs of State* 61–62 (1977).

[98] Globe 685. Without suffrage, said Senator Samuel Pomeroy, the Negro "has no security." Id. 1182.

[99] Id. 3980, 4000.

[100] James 167.

[101] It was a "rather consistent practice . . . to disavow Radical influence in framing of the congressional proposal." Id. The *New York Herald* stated that the Amendment "is not the platform of Thaddeus Stevens, Sumner, or any of the noisy radicals in Congress. They can do nothing. It was adopted against all their remonstrances and in spite of their threats." N.Y. Herald, Sept. 28, 1866, quoted in Benedict, supra note 82 at 198.

Fessendon, co-chairman of the Joint Committee, was "un-willing to allow the process of reconstruction to be con-trolled by the radicals."[102] Taking no notice of these facts, Curtis asserts, "Fairman's belief that antislavery ideas were limited to 'the most radical' Republicans was simply a mis-take."[103] It is Curtis who is mistaken.

[102] Kendrick, supra note 76 at 174.
[103] Curtis, Book 108.

CHAPTER SIX

Some Curtis Misconceptions

LET us now consider Curtis' treatment of specific items of evidence.

THE CIVIL RIGHTS ACT AND THE FOURTEENTH AMENDMENT ARE "IDENTICAL"

Originally Curtis asserted that Stevens "denied that the amendment and the Civil Rights Bill were identical. That was 'only partly true'."[1] I pointed out that this is a misleading version of Stevens' comment on the Fourteenth Amendment: "' Some answer "your civil rights bill secures the same things." That is partly true, but *a law is repealable by a majority*'."[2] But for that solitary exception, Stevens plainly was not repudiating the general opinion that the Act and the Amendment were "identical." Nevertheless, Curtis now repeats that "Stevens, manager of the Fourteenth Amendment in the House, denied that the amendment and the Civil Rights bill were identical. That was, as he said, "'only partly true'."[3] To persist in repeating a palpable half-truth after it has been called to his attention speaks volumes for Curtis' standards of scholarship.

He notes "statements by some congressmen that the

[1] Curtis, *Adventures* 104.
[2] Berger, *Reply* 4 (emphasis added).
[3] Curtis, Book 103.

Amendment incorporated the substantial protections of the Civil Rights Bill," but argues that this excludes the Bill of Rights whereas these provisions are "by ordinary use of language 'laws for security of person and property',"[4] a phrase contained in the Bill. When the legislative history discommodes him, Curtis, though ostensibly leaning on the legislative intention, substitutes his own reading of "ordinary" words.

In yet more strained fashion Curtis argues that the claim that the

> Fourteenth Amendment is absolutely the same as the Civil Rights Bill . . . is absolutely inconsistent with the language of the Fourteenth Amendment. . . . If the amendment had been designed merely to prohibit discrimination in certain rights that states chose to accord their own citizens, then the due process and privileges and immunities clauses would have been superfluous. To say that "no state shall make or enforce any law which shall abridge the privileges or immunities of citizens of the United States, nor shall any state deprive any person of life, liberty, and property without due process of law" is a very odd way of saying that the state is prohibited from discriminating in certain rights it gives its citizens.[5]

That the Fourteenth Amendment seems to Curtis a "very odd" way of expressing the framers' purposes cannot overcome the all but unanimous agreement that the act and the amendment were "identical."[6] Pretending to search for the

[4] Id. 72, 77, 104. For "ordinary" meaning, see infra Chapter 7 text accompanying note 5; and Justice Frankfurter, infra note 7.

[5] Id. 118–19.

[6] Curtis converts the unanimous array of those who considered Bill and Amendment to be identical (supra Chapter 2 text accompanying notes 13–18) into "a few said that the amendment and bill were identical." Curtis, Book 93. This is an improvement on his earlier statement that "*Berger attempts* to tie the privileges and immunities clause of the fourteenth amendment to the Civil Rights Bill and to establish their complete identity." Curtis, *Reply* 8. He simply cannot bring himself to acknowl-

framers' intention, Curtis ignores their explanations when it undermines his thesis.[7]

"Privileges or immunities" were far from "superfluous"; they were words of art[8] that identified the category of rights that were not to be abridged. Justice Harlan, it will be recalled, considered that the privileges or immunities clause was "expected to be the primary source of substantive protection," that the due process and equal protection clauses were "relegated to a secondary rule,"[9] a role I would describe as adjective. The equal protection clause, as its history

---

edge inescapable facts. For emphasis on such "identity" during the Ratification campaign, see supra Chapter 4 text accompanying notes 17–21.

[7] What seems "very odd" to Curtis puzzled the Justices not at all. Led by Justice Field, the four dissenters in Slaughter-House Cases, 83 U.S. (16 Wall.) 36, 96 (1872), stated that "in the first section of the Civil Rights Act Congress has given its interpretation of these terms [privileges or immunities] . . . the right to make and enforce contracts etc." Although the majority construed the phrase more narrowly, it yet stated in comparing Article IV (2) and the Fourteenth Amendment that "there can be little question that . . . the privileges and immunities are the same in each." Id. 75.

Justice Frankfurter stated in his concurring *Adamson* opinion that adoption of the due process clause would be "a strange way of saying" that "every State must thereafter initiate prosecutions through indictment by grand jury, must have a trial by a jury of twelve in criminal cases." 322 U.S. 46, 63 (1947), for which the Fifth and Sixth Amendments made explicit provision. How "very odd" of Curtis to swallow so "strange" a reading.

In similarly strange fashion, Curtis argues that "The claim that the Fourteenth Amendment clearly supplied power to pass the bill, if anything, supports the conclusion that the Amendment was designed to apply the Bill of Rights to the States," relying on "the fact that Wilson, Thayer, and Bingham all analysed the Bill as an attempt to enforce the Bill of Rights, *specifically* the due process clause of the fifth amendment." Curtis, Book 109 (emphasis added). But incorporation of one provision excludes wholesale adoption of all the others. See infra note 43.

[8] Infra Chapter 7 text accompanying note 10.

[9] Oregon v. Mitchell, 400 U.S. 112, 163, 164 (1970).

discloses, embodied the act's prohibition of discrimination with respect to the rights there specified[10]—privileges or immunities. And the due process clause afforded access to the courts for protection of those rights. What is "very odd" about that? Instead of employing the negative "No discrimination" of the Bill, the Amendment offered to blacks the same described rights as whites enjoyed, accompanied by enforcement.

"Suppose," Curtis argues, "the amendment and the bill were 'identical.' If they were, it follows that the Civil Rights Bill included a federal standard of due process."[11] A "federal standard of due process" is a construct of the modern Court, as yet hidden from the minds of the framers.[12] In *Walker v. Sauvinet,* a decision contemporaneous with adoption of the Amendment, the Court declared that due "process in the States is regulated by the law of the States."[13] Next Curtis asserts that "since the bill made all persons born in the United States citizens they would have *all* the rights of citizens, rights that most Republicans who spoke on the subject believed included the protection of the Bill of Rights liberties against infringement by the States."[14] But those liberties were in fact protected only against the federal government, not the States. And Curtis overlooks that the Bill did not merely confer citizenship; it went on to specify certain rights that the newly made citizens would enjoy[15]—

[10] Infra Chapter 8 text accompanying notes 11, 12, 20, 24; see also Berger, *Judiciary* 166–92.

[11] Curtis, Book 104.

[12] See supra Chapter 1 text accompanying notes 20–28.

[13] 92 U.S. 90, 93 (1875). See infra Chapter 8 text accompanying note 95.

[14] Id. 104 (emphasis added). Curtis ignores the framers' repeated rejection of proposals to bar *all* discrimination; see Berger, *Judiciary* 163–164; *infra* Conclusion text accompanying notes 1–3.

[15] Curtis acknowledges that "The Civil Rights Act listed certain specific rights, such as the right to testify and to hold property. These were

justly described by *Georgia v. Rachel* as "a limited category of rights"—and that the Framers repeatedly rejected proposals to prohibit *all* manner of discrimination.[16] The perils of reliance on definitions of citizenship are illustrated by a Democrat's appeal to *Webster's Dictionary* definition of a citizen as one "who had the privilege of exercising the elective franchise."[17] Yet we have it from Senator Jacob Howard, a pivotal Curtis "authority," that "three fourths of the States of this Union could not be induced to vote to *grant* the rights of suffrage . . . to the colored race."[18]

That the grant of "rights" resided in the discretion of the states was made unmistakably clear by Samuel Shellabarger, a vigorous proponent of the Civil Rights Bill:

> if this section did in fact assume to confer or define or regulate these civil rights, which are named by the words contract, sue, testify, inherit, &c., then it would . . . be an assertion of the reserved rights of the States and the people. But, sir, except so far as it confers citizenship, it neither confers nor defines nor regulates any rights whatever. Its whole effect is not to confer

---

rights under local law. It is natural to read the general words in light of the specific ones." Curtis, Book 103. It is more than natural, it is a long-established rule of law: "Specific words prevail over the general in the same or another statute which might otherwise be controlling." Ginsberg & Sons v. Popkin, 285 U.S. 204, 208 (1932). See also Fourco Glass Co. v. Transmirra Products Corp. 353 U.S. 222 (1957); and see infra Chapter 8 note 7, and Madison, 3 Farrand 366.

[16] 384 U.S. 780, 791 (1966); Berger *Judiciary* 163–64; infra Conclusion text accompanying notes 1–3.

[17] Bond 451. Trumbull told the Senate that "the granting of civil rights does not . . . carry with it . . . political privileges. A man may be a citizen in this country without a right to vote. . . . The right to vote . . . depends upon the legislation of the various States." Avins 197.

[18] Avins 220 (emphasis added). In the House, Wilson said that had it "been supposed" that the Thirteenth Amendment authorized Congress to regulate suffrage, "it would never have passed Congress, never have received the sanction of the States." Id. 173.

or regulate rights, but to require that whatever of these enumerated rights and obligations are imposed by State laws shall
be for and upon all citizens alike without distinction based on
race or former condition of slavery.[19]

Curtis finds these remarks "qualified and ambiguous," "as if
[the Bill] merely encompassed equal protection."[20] He forgets the opening phrase of the Bill: "there shall be no discrimination in civil rights and immunities." Although these
words were deleted upon Bingham's insistence that they
were "oppressive" and unduly encroached on the States' domain,[21] the remainder of the Bill shows that the ban on discrimination remained the goal.[22]

Curtis is critical of Shellabarger because he "seems to
have felt that states could continue to refuse to allow mar-
ried women to testify after the passage of the bill. Such a
rule of law seems to be the very denial of due process for-
bidden by the Civil Rights Bill *in the case of blacks* and by the
Fourteenth Amendment in the case of all 'persons'."[23] Since,
however, the Bill outlawed discrimination only on account
of race, it did not apply to women. Speaking to the Fourteenth Amendment, Senator Jacob Howard, one of the pillars of Curtis' thesis, stated that by the "law of nature"
women and children were "not regarded as the equals of
men."[24] At this time it was accepted that a woman's place

[19]Avins 188. Shellabarger also said that the Bill is not meant "to usurp
the powers of the States to punish offenders generally against the rights
of citizens in the several States, but its whole force is expended in defeat-
ing an attempt, under State laws, to deprive races and the members
thereof as such of the rights enumerated in this act. This is the whole of
it." Avins 189.

[20]Curtis, Book 78.

[21]Supra Chapter 2 text accompanying notes 29–32.

[22]Id. text accompanying note 26.

[23]Curtis, Book 78 (emphasis added).

[24]Avins 221.

was in the home. Soon the Court held that the Amendment did not require a State to admit a woman to the Bar.[25]

Against this background Curtis concludes that the "*inescapable* implication of the assertion that the Civil Rights Bill and Section 1 of the Amendment are identical is that at least some of the rights in the Bill of Rights applied to the States prior to the passage of the fourteenth amendment."[26] This makes "identical" turn somersaults. No reference to the Bill of Rights is to be found in the history of the Civil Rights Bill; so Curtis would read back into the Bill "rights" that were first "discovered" in the Amendment by the modern Court. In stating that the Amendment was "identical" with the Bill, the framers merely meant that the Amendment did not go beyond the Bill; they did not intend to expand the scope of the Amendment by identifying the Amendment with the Bill. Bingham's rejection of the "oppressive" ambit of "civil rights and immunities" alone would bar Curtis' unfounded inference.

Finally, when some proponents of the Amendment observed that section 1 simply "reenacts what is already in the Constitution," Bond concluded, "they had in mind the privileges or immunities clause of Article IV rather than the Bill of Rights. There is no record in Pennsylvania, Ohio, or Illinois of any advocate of the 14th amendment explaining that the privileges and immunities clause guaranteed those rights enshrined in the Bill of Rights."[27] One who would argue that silence is equally consistent with incorporation of the Bill of Rights has the burden of proof that the Framers *in-*

---

[25] Bradwell v. State, 83 U.S. (16 Wall.) 130 (1872). Justices Bradley, Swayne, and Field concurring, said, "The natural and proper timidity of and delicacy which belongs to the female sex unfits it for many occupations of civil life." Id. 141.

[26] Curtis, Book 104.

[27] Bond 450.

tended to curtail State sovereignty further by making the Bill of Rights applicable to the States.[28]

SELECTIVE INCORPORATION

Curtis proffers some "historical proof" that the Framers contemplated "selective incorporation":

> I have found over thirty examples of statements by Republicans during the Thirty-eighth and Thirty-ninth Congresses indicating that they believed that *at least some* Bill of Rights liberties limited the States. . . . I found no statements by Republicans indicating that the states were free under a *proper* understanding of the law to violate rights in the Bill of Rights. . . . The often expressed idea that the amendment protected fundamental rights could provide a basis for selective incorporation.[29]

Given Howard Jay Graham's concession that Radical Republican views were "rankly, frankly heretical"—in Curtis' words, "radically unorthodox"[30]—the conversion of the majority is not to be assumed but must be proved. As Leonard Levy wrote in similar case, "there is no reason to believe that Bingham and Howard expressed the views of the majority of Congress."[31] The framers' careful employment of words of art—but for "equal protection"—argues to the contrary. Curtis himself is troubled by their "explicit" provision for some cases but none for incorporation of the Bill of Rights.[32]

Let us consider Curtis' arguments seriatim. That some

[28] See supra Chapter 5 text accompanying notes 42–46; and see Judge Posner, supra Chapter 1 note 55.

[29] Curtis, Book 112 (emphasis added).

[30] Id. 126; see also supra Chapter 5 notes 93, 95, 100; infra Chapter 7 text accompanying note 46.

[31] L. Levy, *Judgments: Essays on American Constitutional History* 77 (1972).

[32] Infra Chapter 7 text accompanying notes 48–54.

Republicans thought "some Bill of Rights liberties limited the States" raises the question "did the speakers agree on *which* "liberties"? Among the abolitionists, upon whom Curtis heavily relies, there was general agreement, tenBroek found, only about the due process clause and the First and Fourth Amendments.[33] TenBroek denied that "all abolitionists put forward *all* the first eight emendments to combat all phases of slavery. . . . They certainly did not."[34] Nor may we deduce a general agreement that future interpreters would be left selectively to incorporate their favorite provisions. Of such an agreement there is no hint.

Curtis' appeal to "fundamental rights" as a basis for "selective incorporation" stands no better. "Fundamental rights," as will appear, were associated by those who explained the Civil Rights Bill with the "limited category" of rights protected against discrimination by that Bill, not by the Bill of Rights.[35] What could be a more "proper" understanding of the law than the Supreme Court's long-standing decision in *Barron v. Baltimore* that the Bill of Rights does not apply to the States? Nonabolitionist lawyers familiar with Chief Justice Marshall's opinion, read to them by Bingham,[36] had no occasion to question whether the States were free to violate a law that did not apply to them. Then too, Curtis' two bellwethers, Senators Howard and Bingham, whose views, Curtis considers, "are entitled to very great weight,"[37] read against selective incorporation. Howard stated that "to these privileges and immunities . . . should be added the personal

[33] Jacobus tenBroek, *Equal Under Law* 127 (1965). The "rights in the other amendments," tenBroek wrote, "received only casual, incidental, and infrequent reference." Id. 127.

[34] Id. 126–27.

[35] Infra Chapter 8 text accompanying notes 1–41.

[36] Avins 157, 158.

[37] Curtis, Book 120.

rights guaranteed and secured by the first eight amendments."[38] Curtis recognizes that "Howard's speech mili-
tated strongly in the direction of full incorporation."[39] Bingham referred to "this immortal bill of rights," and asked, "Is
the bill of rights to stand in our Constitution . . . a mere
dead letter?"[40] Curtis considers that Bingham referred to
"the first eight amendments."[41] Here is still another conflict,
between those who were for full incorporation and those
who spoke of differing select rights, a conflict that renders
the several Republican remarks inconclusive evidence of
"original intention." On the basis of this melange Curtis
charges Judge Friendly with "disregard [of] virtually all the
evidence"![42]

In truth, the framers did their own selective incorporation. Out of the Bill of Rights they selected and incorporated the due process clause in the Fourteenth Amendment;
and under the long-established rule that mention of *A* excludes the unmentioned *B,* reinforced by the Joint Committee's rejection of the just compensation clause of the Bill of
Rights,[43] they thus barred attribution to them of an intention to license selective incorporation of other items of the
Bill of Rights.

[38] Avins 219.
[39] Curtis, Book III.
[40] Avins, 150, 158.
[41] Curtis, Book IIO.
[42] Id. II2.
[43] *Expressio unius est exclusio alterius,* United States v. Arredondo, 31
U.S. (6 Pet.) 691, 725 (1832). In the Pennsylvania Ratification Convention,
James Wilson said that if "the enumeration is not complete, everything
not expressly mentioned will be presumed to be purposely omitted." 3
Max Farrand, *Records of the Federal Convention of 1787* 144 (1911). Egbert
Benson said in the First Congress, "it cannot be rationally intended that
all offices shall be held by good behavior, because the Constitution had
declared one office to be held by this tenure." 1 *Annals of Congress* 505; and
see Alexander White, id. 517. See infra Chapter 8 note 8.

The Fourteenth Amendment as a Criminal Code

We have seen James Wilson's assurance, for example, that "we are not making a general criminal code for the States."[44] Curtis comments that a "code specifies offenses such as larceny and fornication."[45] Let a code of criminal procedure suffice. Judge Henry Friendly entitled his critique, "The Bill of Rights as a Code of Criminal Procedure."[46] Justice Frankfurter wrote that the Fourteenth Amendment "is not the basis of a uniform code of criminal procedure federally imposed."[47] To Fairman's argument that the "country would not have tolerated having the 'federal provisions on grand jury, criminal jury . . . fastened on them in 1866," Curtis retorts that it "ignores the realities of the political process," because the 1866 campaign "dealt with gut issues," e.g., "the political power of the rebellious southern states, racism, and protection for loyalists in the South. Those were issues that could and did defeat politicians. No politician . . . is likely to be defeated for advocating grand juries, criminal juries of twelve," etc. Fairman's argument, he continues, "assumes that Republicans in state legislatures would allow the South

---

For Curtis, rejection of the just compensation proposal by the Joint Committee does not rank nearly as high as Howard's intimation that the Amendment "would overturn court decisions holding that the states could take private property . . . without just compensation. Finally, American courts . . . had held that the law of the land clause or due process clause of state constitutional law prohibited taking without just compensation." Curtis, Book 85. His preference for what Howard "implied" over the vote of the Joint Committee of both Houses illustrates how he tailors his cloth to fit his thesis.

[44] Globe 1120. See also Shellabarger, supra note 19; Bingham, supra Chapter 2 text accompanying note 29.

[45] Curtis, Book 125.

[46] 55 Calif. L. Rev. 929 (1965).

[47] Felix Frankfurter, *Law and Politics* 192–93 (1939).

a dramatic increase of political power by counting disenfranchised blacks for the purposes of representation rather than provide for jury trials in civil cases where the damages exceed twenty dollars. Politicians do not behave in this fashion."[48] This sets up a false issue and a false antithesis. Local control over criminal administration was and remains a "gut" issue, witness continuing adherence to the States' death penalties notwithstanding the Court's crusade to abolish and hobble them. Curtis would be hard-pressed to name one Northern "politician" who openly preferred federal to State control of criminal and civil administration in his own State.[49] Nor was the North faced by a choice between a federal takeover of local criminal administration and a contraction of Southern representation geared to black disenfranchisement. For the latter, §2 provided for a pro rata diminution of representation, while §1 provided for a due process trial which Northerners desired to secure to Southern blacks. Politicians were not faced by a distressing choice between the two; they were in tandem. The issue, rather, is whether the North was apprised that the Amendment called upon it to surrender State control of criminal administration.

SECURITY OF PERSON AND PROPERTY

Curtis sets great store on the penultimate clause of the Civil Rights Bill—"equal benefit of all laws and proceedings for

[48] Curtis, Book 105.

[49] Justice Frankfurter, concurring in Adamson v. California, 332 U.S. 46, 64 (1947), stated, "It could hardly have occurred to these States [which had no rigorous grand jury requirement] that by ratifying the Amendment they had uprooted their established methods of prosecuting crime and fastened upon themselves a new prosecutorial system." Chief Justice Chase feared that "Even loyal people in the Northern States . . . might oppose the amendment because of its threat to states rights." James 118. See supra Shellabarger note 19, and Chapter 5 text accompanying notes 23–32.

the security of person and property." He insists that the "provisions of the Bill of Rights are, by ordinary use of language, 'laws for security of person and property'."[50] Now the guarantee of "security of person and property" responded to the "acts of cruelty, oppression and murder" whereby the South terrorized the freedmen.[51] Such offenses gave rise to rights under *State* law as Bingham recognized.[52] Existing "law" held the Bill of Rights inapplicable to the States, so it is idle to invoke the "ordinary use of language," a treacherous guide to legal terms. "Law" does not mean dissenting abolitionist opinion.

Then there is Bingham's insistence that State sovereignty demanded deletion of the words "civil rights," which followed in order to forestall a "latitudinarian construction not intended."[53] To make "security of person and property" the vehicle of that very construction would be to kick the devil out the door and let him return through the window. Courts will avoid an unreasonable construction, one that is plainly at war with the purpose of the draftsmen.[54] Again, Shellabarger stated that the "right to contract, sue, testify, &c." was "necessary" for the "protection of the rights of person and property."[55] Such specification was superfluous if "security of person and property" embraced the specified rights and more. Then too, "Thayer said that the rights enumerated in the Civil Rights bill 'preclude[d] extension of the gen-

---

[50] Curtis, Book 72; id. 77, 104.

[51] See supra Chapter 2 note 19.

[52] Bingham, supra Chapter 2 text accompanying note 45. See Hamilton supra Chapter 2 note 29.

[53] Supra Chapter 2 text accompanying notes 29–31.

[54] North American Utility Securities Corp. v. Posen, 176 F. 2d 194, 196 (3d Cir. 1949). Wilson stated that his "amendment strikes out *all* of these general terms." Supra Chapter 2 text accompanying note 31 (emphasis added).

[55] Avins 188.

eral words beyond the particulars which [have] been enumerated'."[56] Curtis would distinguish this on two grounds:
(1) Thayer was engaged in denying that the words "civil
rights and immunities" included "the state law right to
vote." The deletion of the "civil rights" phrase and enumeration of specified rights rendered it unnecessary to state that
other rights were excluded. (2) While asking why "*these* fundamental rights" should not be extended to the freedmen,
Thayer concluded "why should they not have full and equal
benefit of all laws and proceedings for the security of person
and property."[57] The reasonable inference is that Thayer
considered that "laws and proceedings for the security of
person and property" were synonymous with "*these* fundamental rights." Thayer was not expressly circumscribing
one generality only to replace it by an even more unlimited
one, as Wilson confirmed: "To obviate . . . *any* other construction *beyond the specific* rights named in the section, our
amendment strikes out *all* of those general terms and leaves
the bill with the rights specified in the section."[58] Although
the penultimate clause was not physically stricken, the intention to confine the Bill to the specified words governs.
Curtis, it will be recalled, summons the original intention
for his thesis.

Consider Curtis' paraphrase of William Lawrence's comment on the Civil Rights Bill that "citizens have certain absolute rights including personal security, personal property,
and liberty, and that the Bill of Rights declared that no person should be deprived of life, liberty, or property without

[56] Curtis, Book 79.

[57] Id. 79–80 (emphasis in original).

[58] Avins 191 (emphasis added). Curtis notes that "John Thomas, like a
number of his colleagues, sought to ensure for blacks the rights to acquire and dispose of personal and real property, to testify, and to have

just compensation."[59] What weight can be attached to this in light of the Joint Committee's rejection of Bingham's motion to add to the Amendment the clause "nor take private property for public use without just compensation."[60] Here we have an unimpeachable fact, and Curtis consumes a page to explain the fact away setting forth some complicated suppositions to demonstrate that the "rejection proves nothing except at the time it was submitted the committee found the form of Bingham's proposal deficient."[61] He would rob the unequivocal rejection of meaning by sheer speculation. That the rejection went beyond "form" is attested by the fact that "just compensation" never did find its way into the amendment. And the rejection of "just compensation" again testifies that the framers were loath to interfere with control over local matters beyond the "limited category" set forth in the Civil Rights Act. Late in the discussion of the Amendment, Senator James Patterson, who voted for it, declared, "I am opposed to any law discriminating against them [blacks] in the security and protection of life, liberty, person and property, and the proceeds of their labor. Beyond this I am not prepared to go."[62] Plainly Patterson, unlike Curtis, did not understand life, liberty, and property to be of unbounded scope.[63]

---

their life, liberty, and property protected by the same laws that protected whites." Curtis, Book 54. Whites were not protected against State action by the Bill of Rights.

[59] Curtis, Book 77.

[60] Id. 84; Bickel 42.

[61] Curtis, Book 84.

[62] Globe 2699.

[63] For similar remarks, see Berger, *Judiciary* 170–71. As has been noted, the framers meant to "protect" the blacks from outrage, terror, and oppression, supra Chapter 2 note 119; Chapter 4 note 9; infra text accompanying notes 75–76.

RATIFICATION DEBATE

Curtis devotes a chapter—"The Amendment Before the States"—to the subject. He takes no account of Senator Sherman's statement in September 1866 to a Cincinnati audience that "we defeated every radical proposition in it."[64] Nor does he notice the statement in the *New York Herald* of September 28, 1866, that the Amendment "is not the platform of Thaddeus Stevens, Sumner, or any of the noisy radicals in Congress. They can do nothing. It was adopted against all their remonstrances and in spite of their threats."[65] It was, said Joseph James, a "rather consistent practice . . . to disavow all Radical influence in the framing of the congressional proposal."[66] Earlier the *Chicago Tribune,* a Radical paper, considered that the proposed Amendment "might be a good election platform even if it failed to represent Radical principles."[67] Bond, echoing Benedict, observed that "Radicals did not control the Republican party. Having failed to shape the amendment entirely to their liking, the radicals accepted §1 as a compromise."[68] For this we need go no further than Curtis' oft-cited Radical, Senator Yates, who said of the Amendment, "we have the medium between extremes . . . If we do not meet the views of the Radicals . . . we have at all events the medium, the moderation which has been agreed upon."[69] These statements should dispose of Curtis' reliance on the "beliefs" of some Radicals in the "frankly, rankly heretical" abolitionist views.

Curtis notes a "common theme in messages by the gover-

[64] James 167.
[65] M. L. Benedict, *A Compromise With Principle* 198 (1975).
[66] James 167.
[67] Id. 134.
[68] Bond 453.
[69] Avins 237.

nors was that the amendment would protect the 'rights' or
'liberty' of citizens in the United States," but remarks that
the "messages are silent on exactly what rights the governors thought were encompassed by the phrase 'rights of
citizens of the United States'." Except for the governors' insistence that "the amendment would protect liberty," they
"failed to discuss its legal effect."[70] But this is of no moment, he claims, because "the messages are fully consistent
with an intent to apply the Bill of Rights to the States. To
read the messages as inconsistent with that goal, one has to
assume that references to the 'rights of citizens of the United
States,' or to 'liberty' exclude the liberties in the Bill of
Rights."[71]

Curtis erroneously shifts the burden of proof. He would
require critics of incorporation to prove the negative—that
the terms do not include the Bill of Rights—before he
proves the intention to incorporate it. Since application of
the Bill of Rights to the States drastically curtails the right
of the Northern States to control their own internal affairs,
that purpose has to be proved, not assumed. What Chief
Justice Marshall said of such "extraordinary" intervention
remains true today: had the 1866 framers contemplated it
"they would have declared their purpose in plain and intelligible language."[72] In an opinion contemporary with adoption of the Fourteenth Amendment, Justice Miller rejected
a construction that would subject State "to the control of
Congress, in the exercise of powers heretofore universally
conceded to them" in the absence of "language which expresses such a purpose too clearly to admit of doubt."[73]

Curtis' argument is replete with citations to the "pursuit

[70] Curtis, Book 146–47.
[71] Id. 147.
[72] Supra Chapter 1 text accompanying note 9.
[73] Slaughter-House Cases, 83 U.S. (16 Wall.) 36, 78 (1872).

of happiness,"[74] which in his hands becomes an overflowing cornucopia. "Protection" was not a vague abstraction for the North; it spelled protection against flogging and outrage in the South.[75] Let Curtis' own witness, William D. Kelley, speak: "Northerners could go South," Kelley said, "but once there 'they could not express their thoughts as freemen and receive the protection they were entitled to as citizens of the Republic'."[76] Nor was "liberty" enigmatic, but as stump speakers were apt to explain, it meant "the right of locomotion, the right to go where they please . . . and own property where they please,"[77] made necessary by the Black Codes which would chain blacks to their hovels.[78]

It serves no useful purpose to beat a tattoo on the phrase "pursuit of happiness"[79] without explaining what it embraces. "Happiness" obviously is a protean term; one man's meat is another man's poison. It means one thing to rock music fans who flock to a multidecibel discotheque and something else again to the luckless neighbors. Realizing that "happiness" is too vague to be enforceable, Justices Field and Bradley sought to tie it to identifiable rights. Field declared that by "the right of men to pursue happiness" is "meant the right to pursue any lawful business or vocation."[80] Bradley stated, "The right to follow any of the common occupations of life is an undeniable right; it was formulated as such under the phrase 'pursuit of happiness' in

[74] Curtis, Book 117, 132, 142–49.

[75] Bond 443, 449; Avins 131, 199; supra Chapter 4 note 9.

[76] Curtis, Book 138. "The failure of the Southern state governments to protect the freedman had outraged the Unionists." Bond 448.

[77] Bond 448; see also Wilson, supra Chapter 2 text accompanying note 24.

[78] For brutal examples, see Avins, 95, 109, 121, 135, 136, 149, 168, 171, 199.

[79] Curtis, Book 117, 132, 142, 149.

[80] Butchers' Union Co. v. Crescent City Co., 111 U.S. 746, 757 (1884).

the Declaration of Independence."[81] It is food for thought
that with the "pursuit of happiness" before them, the Framers clung to the traditional triad—"life, liberty, and property." For they were bent on safeguarding the "protection"
of person and property,[82] nothing more.

Curtis' citations do not compel a contrary conclusion.
Columbus Delano said in Ohio on August 31, 1866, that §1

> provides that the privileges and immunities of these citizens
> shall not be destroyed or impaired by state legislation, and it
> provides that no man shall be deprived of life, liberty, and
> property without due process of law. . . . I know very well that
> the citizen of the South and of the North going South have not
> hitherto been safe in the South, for want of constitutional
> power . . . to protect them.[83]

Delano confirms that the mischief was violence in the South,
from which citizens must be protected—protection in its
primary, concrete sense—save the freedman from lynch-
ing. Delano, moreover, was opposed to conferring upon
blacks "the right of being jurors"; and he did "not believe
that the rights of the States are utterly overwhelmed and dethroned."[84] In fact, he inveighed against an authority to "go
into the States and manage and legislate with regard to all
the personal rights of the citizens—rights of life, liberty and
property."[85]

Another Curtis witness is "General John Alexander Logan, Republican candidate for congressman-at-large from
Illinois," who "suggested that the rights of citizens include

[81] Id. at 762.
[82] See, e.g., Windom, Avins 171; supra text accompanying notes 75–77.
Madison's proposed Bill of Rights had a "happiness" phrase, but it did
not survive. 1 *Annals of Congress* 434.
[83] Curtis, Book 138–39.
[84] Avins 177–78.
[85] Id. 179.

the right to own property, to sue, and to protection of life, liberty and property."[86] William Gillette considers that he was "a wily Republican politician from anti-Negro southern Illinois," who "wanted to scrap the Negro office-holding guarantee, no doubt accurately reflecting the will of his constituency,"[87] and who said, "The Negro equality talk against the amendment is all a bugbear and humbug. I don't consider a 'nigger' my equal."[88] Thus Logan is a most unlikely witness for a broad construction of the Amendment.

Then there is Senator Richard Yates of Illinois, who asked, "Do you suppose any of you can go south and express your sentiments freely and in safety? No . . . We will rally around the flag, shouting the battle cry of freedom." His remarks, Curtis recounts, "were met 'with tremendous applause'."[89] Earlier, Yates had proposed that "No State . . . shall . . . in any manner recognize *any* distinction . . . on account of race," but was decisively voted down, 38 to 7.[90] Notwithstanding, he voted for the amendment as the counsel of

[86] Curtis, Book 131, 132.

[87] William Gillette, *The Right to Vote: Politics and the Passage of the Fifteenth Amendment* 68 (1965).

[88] Bond 467. Bond notes that "Illinois, Indiana, Iowa, and Ohio prohibited or severely restricted Negro migration and settlement within their boundaries." Id. 441 note 33. Senator Sherman stated in 1867 in Ohio, "we do not like Negroes; we do not conceal our dislike." C. V. Woodward, "Seeds of Failure in Radical Race Policy," in *New Frontiers of the American Reconstruction* 128 (H. Hyman ed. 1966). Senator Henry Wilson, a Massachusetts Radical, acknowledged that "There is not a square mile in the United States where the equal rights and privileges of the colored man has not been in the past and is not now unpopular." Cong. Globe, 40th Cong., 3d Sess. 672 (1869). Bond observes that the "Democrats chose to run 'against the nigger'"; and Republicans were constrained to "diffuse the racist attack." Bond 441, 442.

[89] Curtis, Book 138.

[90] Globe App. 98; Globe 1287 (emphasis added).

moderation, even though it did "not meet the views of the Radicals."[91] He was well aware that "the moderation which has been agreed on"[92] overcame any Radical speeches to the contrary. Thus Curtis' own witnesses undermine rather than advance his cause. And his incessant reiteration of generalities is oblivious to the truth encapsulated by Justice Frankfurter: "It's the details that determine judgment. Generalities don't amount to a hill of beans."[93]

Barron v. Baltimore

Chief Justice Marshall held in *Barron v. Baltimore,* it will be recalled, that the Bill of Rights did not apply to the States. Curtis' chief authority, John Bingham, recognized that "*as ruled* the existing amendments are not applicable to and do not bind the States."[94] Curtis states, however, that "leading Republicans believed that the Bill of Rights were [sic] already binding on the States,"[95] although he notes Republicans' recognition that their views were unorthodox.[96] And some believed that a constitutional amendment was required to correct *Barron v. Baltimore,*[97] a conflict of opinion to say the least.

Curtis avers that Bingham "did not agree that *Barron v. Baltimore* had been correctly decided" because he "believed the States were required to obey the Bill of Rights *by the oath* state officers took to support the Constitu-

---

[91] Avins 237.
[92] Id.
[93] Harlan B. Phillips, *Felix Frankfurter Reminisces* 198 (1960).
[94] Avins 158.
[95] Curtis, Book 124.
[96] Id. 52; see also supra text accompanying note 31.
[97] Curtis, Book 233 note 201.

tion."[98] This is a pretty example of circular reasoning. Only if the States were bound by the Bill of Rights did the "oath" come into play. Hence, Crosskey tells us, "Bingham actually drew" a draft of §1 of the Amendment "upon the assumption that his own constitutional ideas and those of [some of] his Republican brethren and *not* the Supreme Court's constitutional decisions, were the standing law."[99] One may not assume that the framers overruled a constitutional decision sub silentio. When they deemed it necessary to overrule *Dred Scott,* the framers, Curtis notices, "explicitly wrote national citizenship . . . into the fourteenth amendment."[100]

In truth, Bingham was utterly confused as to what *Barron v. Baltimore* held. He believed, Curtis tells us, "that the rights in the Bill of Rights were protected from state infringement by the privileges and immunities clause of article IV, section 2. Still he was aware of decisions like Barron v. Baltimore to the contrary."[101] *Barron,* however, held that the Bill of Rights did not apply to the States; it said nothing whatsoever about Article IV. That Article, moreover, had nothing to do with the Bill of Rights, which came into being after the Constitution was adopted. And it provided only that visitors from a sister State should enjoy cer-

[98] Curtis, *Adventures* 100.

[99] William Crosskey, "Charles Fairman's 'Legislative History' and the Constitutional Limitations on State Authority," 22 U. Chi. L. Rev. 25 (1954) (emphasis in original). Among the "several defects" contained in Bingham's proposal of February 26, 1866, Curtis remarks, was "the assumption that Bingham's views and those of a number of his colleagues, not the decisions of the Supreme Court, accurately stated the law. The proposal assumed without providing explicitly that contrary to *Dred Scott* free blacks were citizens of the United States." Curtis, Book 62–63.

[100] Curtis, *Adventures* 97.

[101] Curtis, Book 61.

tain rights of a resident in the host State. Under *Barron* the resident himself did not enjoy the protection of the federal Bill of Rights.

SECTION 5 OF THE FOURTEENTH AMENDMENT

Curtis would rob §5 of the Fourteenth Amendment of its meaning. "Republicans," he writes, "repeatedly said that the passage of the amendment put enforcement of its principles beyond the power of congressional majorities. These statements clearly presuppose *judicial enforcement*."[102] The Amendment, to be sure, disabled future congressional majorities from *repealing* its principles. But its §5 provides that "The *Congress* shall have *power to enforce* by appropriate legislation the provisions of this article." And in 1879 the Supreme Court declared that

> It is not said that the judicial power . . . shall extend to enforcing the prohibitions and protecting the rights and immunities guaranteed. . . . *Congress* is authorized to enforce the prohibitions by appropriate legislation."[103]

[102] Id. 130 (emphasis added).

[103] *Ex parte* Virginia, 100 U.S. 339, 345 (1879). Joseph James concluded that "there was little inclination to bestow new powers on the judiciary, but rather to lean on augmented power of Congress." James 184. Henry Monaghan wrote, "I am unable to believe that in light of the then prevailing concepts of representative democracy, the framers or ratifiers of §1 intended the *courts* (rather than the national legislature pursuant to §5) to weave the tapestry of federally protected rights against state government." H. Monaghan, "The Constitution Goes to Harvard," 13 Harv. C.R. & C.L. L. Rev. 113, 124 (1978).

Curtis' citations do not pretend to counter these pronouncements. Curtis, Book 251 note 295. Thus Garfield merely stated that the Amendment would place the Civil Rights Bill beyond the possibility of repeal, put it "above the reach of political strife." Avins 213. Senator Howard explained that it was the purpose of the Amendment "to give validity" to "Constitutional power to enact" the Bill. Avins 228. Neither citation has the remotest relevance to judicial enforcement.

The literal terms of §5 are confirmed by Reconstruction history. Senator Oliver Morton adverted in 1872 to the "great fact" that "the remedy for violation of the Fourteenth and Fifteenth Amendments was expressly not left to the courts. The remedy was legislative, because in each the amendment itself provided that it shall be enforced by legislation."[104] The reason is not far to seek. From at least *Dred Scott* onward the Court was in ill repute. Bingham stated that the Court had "dared to descend from its high place in the discussion and judgment of purely judicial questions to the settlement of political questions which it has no more right to decide for the American people than has the Court of St. Petersburg."[105]

[104] Cong. Globe, 42d Cong., 2d Sess., 525 (1872). For additional citations, see R. Berger, "The Fourteenth Amendment: Light From the Fifteenth," 74 Nw. U.L. Rev. 311, 351 note 242 (1979). Curtis states, "Berger *argued* that the amendment was to be enforced by Congress only, not the courts." Curtis, Book 128, again reducing incontrovertible facts to "Berger argues." (Emphasis added.) Of course, Congress could delegate enforcement of its legislation to the courts.

[105] 6 Charles Fairman, *History of the Supreme Court of the United States*, 462 (1971).

CHAPTER SEVEN

Of "Privileges or Immunities"

THE argument that the framers of the Fourteenth Amendment intended by the "privileges or immunities" clause to incorporate the Bill of Rights is central to Curtis' thesis. He conceded that his "thesis is intensely controversial. It has never for instance been accepted by the United States Supreme Court."[1] And he confessed that it is "difficult to show that Republicans read the original privileges clause [of Article IV (2)] to require the states to obey the Bill of Rights."[2] His goal was to find the "probable Republican understanding of a question to which they devoted comparatively little direct attention."[3]

Curtis approaches "privileges or immunities" with some individual theories of construction. He considers that the words are "a natural way to describe the rights in a Bill of Rights."[4] On the other hand, Justice Frankfurter declared, "Those reading the English language with the meaning it ordinarily conveys . . . would hardly recognize the Fourteenth Amendment as a cover for the various explicit provisions of the first eight amendments."[5] The explicit adoption of one phrase—due process—from the eight amendments

[1] Curtis, Book 2.
[2] Curtis, *Reply* 57.
[3] Curtis, Book 15–16.
[4] Curtis, *Reply* 48.
[5] Adamson v. California, 332 U.S. 46, 63 (1947).

would lead a reader to ask why such particularity if all eight were tacitly adopted. Bingham explained that he drew the terms from Article IV(2) of the original Constitution.[6] Since the Bill of Rights was added later, Article IV (2) could not comprehend the as yet unborn. Disregard of these differences leads Curtis to say that James Garfield "believed that the Bill of Rights limited the States," quoting Garfield's "citizens of each State shall be entitled to all the privileges and immunities of citizens in the several States,"[7] the language of Article IV (2), *not* of the Bill of Rights. Nor did Trumbull indulge in a "natural" reading. Instead, he first read the relevant judicial constructions and said in lawyer-like fashion, "this being *the construction as settled by* judicial decisions."[8] And William Lawrence "concede[d] that the Courts [citing *Abbott* and *Corfield*] have by construction *limited* the words 'all privileges' to mean only '*some* privileges'."[9] In modern terminology, the terms had become "words of art." The Supreme Court stated in similar case, "we should not assume that Congress . . . used the words . . . in their ordinary dictionary meaning when they had already been construed as terms of art carrying a special and limited connotation."[10] By substituting his "natural" meaning for their technical connotation, Curtis is changing the rules to suit his needs.

Curtis' rejection of facts that do not fit his preconceived notions is strikingly exemplified by his treatment of the question whether Article IV (2) was confined to migrants

[6] Curtis, Book 57, 62. So he was understood by William Higby, a Radical; he thought that Article IV (2) and the Fifth Amendment due process clause constituted "precisely what will be provided" by the Bingham amendment. Avins 152.

[7] Curtis, Book 51–52.

[8] Avins 122 (emphasis added).

[9] Id. 207 (emphasis added).

[10] Yates v. United States, 354 U.S. 298, 319 (1957).

from another State. He frames the issue by paraphrasing what *Berger*

> *believed* to be the conventional understanding. . . . The clause was [Berger] *asserted,* not intended to control the powers of state governments over the rights of their citizens, but simply to ensure that a migrant citizen would enjoy the basic rights a state accorded to its citizens. . . . Because blacks were not usually migrants, the clause as conventionally understood, was of no help to them.[11]

It was not merely Berger who alone "believed" and "asserted."

The antecedent of Article IV (2) was Article IV of the Articles of Confederation, which provided for "free ingress and regress to and from any other state." Passing on Article IV (2) of the Constitution, *Abbott v. Bayley* declared that it "can be applied only in cases of removal from one State to another."[12] *Corfield* likewise referred to "[t]he right of a citizen of one State to pass through, or to reside in, any other States."[13] Senator Trumbull advised the Senate that the cases "relate *entirely* to the rights which a citizen in one State has on going into another State, and *not to the rights* of the citizen *belonging to the State.*"[14] As Curtis notes, William Lawrence stated, "citizens removing from one State to another 'were entitled to the privileges that persons . . . are entitled to in the State to which the removal is made'."[15] Two contemporary decisions confirm this understanding. *Paul v. Virginia* said that Article IV (2) gives to citizens of one State the "right of free ingress into other States, and egress from them."[16] Shortly thereafter, the *Slaughter-House*

---

[11] Curtis, Book 114 (emphasis added).
[12] Supra Chapter 3 text accompanying note 10.
[13] Supra Chapter 3 text accompanying note 14.
[14] Avins 137 (emphasis added).
[15] Curtis, Book 77.
[16] 75 U.S. 168, 180 (1868).

Cases quoted from *Corfield* that Article IV (2) threw around privileges and immunities "no security for the citizen of the State in which they were claimed and exercised. . . . Its *sole purpose*" was to prevent discrimination against *out-of-State* citizens with respect to rights granted to its own citizens.[17] Although Justice Field dissented from the narrow view of the majority of five in the *Slaughter-House Cases* respecting the scope of "privileges or immunities," he too observed that what Article IV "did for the protection of the citizens of one State against the hostile and discriminating legislation of other States," the "fourteenth amendment does for the protection of every citizen of the United States against hostile and discriminating legislation against him in favor of others, whether they reside in the same or different States."[18] To disparage such undeniable facts by labeling them "Berger's 'beliefs' and 'assertions'," and by prejudicially asserting that *Dred Scott,* of course, had limited the clause to protection of temporary visitors from another State,"[19] is deplorable advocacy. It was precisely because Article IV (2) did not protect the *resident* emancipated black that the privileges or immunities clause of the Fourteenth Amendment was made applicable to a citizen of the United States. A leading Democratic opponent, Senator Garrett Davis, understood this full well and therefore proposed to substitute the Article IV (2) formula, explaining that it would apply "only where a citizen of one State goes into another State," whereas, he said, Senator Trumbull "proposes now to apply this bill . . . where the citizen is domiciled in the State where he was born."[20]

[17] 83 U.S. (16 Wall.) 36, 77 (1872) (emphasis added).
[18] Id. 100–01.
[19] Curtis, Book 68.
[20] Globe, 595, 596.

Against this Curtis argues that

> Bingham and others who framed the Fourteenth Amendment
> relied on a reading of the privileges and immunities clause of
> Article IV, section 2 by which it protected a body of national
> privileges and immunities of citizens of the United States, in-
> cluding those in the Bill of Rights. This reading may have been
> incorrect.[21]

Curtis compounds Bingham's muddleheadedness, for he
cites to *Barron v. Baltimore* for "incorrect."[22] *Barron,* however, made no reference to Article IV (2) but held that the
Bill of Rights did not apply to the States. Nor could the Article comprehend the Bill of Rights because that came into
existence after adoption of the Constitution. "Incorrect" or
not, Curtis opines, "it does not matter . . . because in the
redrafting of Bingham's first proposal, the amendment *was
rewritten* to secure privileges and immunities of a citizen of
the United States from State abridgement."[23] "Rewriting,"
however, underscores that abolitionist assumptions were incorrect and that deficiencies therefore had to be rectified.[24]
Explicit provision, therefore, did not ratify prior incorrect
assumptions.

Curtis recounts that Bingham had written an early version of the Amendment "on the assumption that his consti-

[21] Curtis, Book 114.

[22] Id. 264 note 151.

[23] Id. 114 (emphasis added). Curtis recounts, "The final version of section 1 was rewritten to incorporate this understanding explicitly." Id. 113.

[24] The Radical Thaddeus Stevens knew that the Constitution "is not a
limitation on the States. The amendment supplies that defect." Curtis,
Book 86. On behalf of the four dissenters in *Slaughter-House Cases* who
argued for a broader construction of "privileges or immunities," Justice
Field stated that by virtue of the Fourteenth Amendment, "A citizen of a
State *is now* only a citizen of the United States residing in that State. The
fundamental rights . . . *now* belong to him as a citizen of the United
States." 83 U.S. at 95 (emphasis added). See Field, *supra* text accompany-
ing note 18.

tutional theories and those of a number of his colleagues, not the decisions of the Supreme Court, were the law of the land,"[25] an assumption that his hard-headed colleagues Trumbull and Fessenden hardly shared.[26] When the drafts-men adopted "citizen of the United States" they did not en-dorse Bingham's flawed premise. Rather they dismissed his "unorthodox" assumptions by employing specific terms to remedy an undeniable lack. They turned from the privileges of "a citizen of each State" to those of a "citizen of the United States," and all the wishful thinking of Bingham & Co. cannot make the same what they were at pains to differ-entiate.[27] For they made persons born in the United States citizens both of "the United States and of the State wherein they reside." Whatever the private meaning that Bingham attached to terms he confessedly borrowed from Article IV

[25] Curtis, *Reply* 66. Yet "Bingham explicitly noted the case of Barron v. Baltimore to show why his amendment was required." Curtis, Book 101.

[26] "A heavy phalanx of Republican politicos, including Sherman and Trumbull . . . were states rights nationalists, suspicious of any new func-tional path the nation travelled." H. M. Hyman, *A More Perfect Union* 312 (1973). Curtis himself acknowledges that Bingham's "assumption" was a "defect." Curtis, Book 62–63.

[27] Slaughter-House Cases, 83 U.S. (16 Wall.) 36, 74 (1872), declared that "a citizenship of the United States and a citizenship of a State . . . are dis-tinct from each other." That distinction eluded Bingham: "The amend-ment is *exactly* in the language of the Constitution; that is to say, it se-cures to the citizens of *each* of the States all the privileges and immunities of citizens of the *several* States. . . . It is to secure to the citizen of each State all the privileges and immunities of citizens of the *United States* in the several States." Avins 160 (emphasis added). Curtis' statement that "Even Berger believed that the privileges and immunities clause of the Fourteenth Amendment went beyond the conventional judicial inter-pretation of Article IV," Curtis, Book 127, must be confined to the sub-stitution of "citizen of the United States" for the earlier "citizen of the several States." The narrow judicial interpretation of the *scope* of the privi-leges and immunities clause was left untouched. Giles Hotchkiss, a New York Radical . . . believed the privileges or immunities section was iden-tical to the guaranty already in the Constitution." Curtis, Book 71. See

and the Fifth Amendment, it cannot overcome the "settled" meaning Trumbull called to the attention of the framers.[28] In evaluating the shift from the Article IV "citizen of each State" to "citizen of the United States," it bears emphasis that the latter phrase was employed, as Senator Trumbull explained, "to end that very controversy, whether the negro is a citizen or not."[29] It was not designed to broaden the scope of "privileges or immunities." So the Court declared in a decision contemporary with the adoption of the Amendment: "The amendment did not add to the privileges and immunities of a citizen. It simply furnished an additional guaranty for the protection of such as he already had."[30] We are indebted to Curtis for a fascinating glimpse of the operation of Bingham's mind. He calls our attention to

> go read, if you please, the words of the Constitution itself: [Article IV (2)] "the citizens of each State (being *ipso facto* citizens of the United States), shall be entitled to all the privileges and immunities of citizens (*supplying the ellipsis* of the United States) in the several States."[31]

What a charmingly simple method of constitutional revision; no more tortured rationalizations—simply "supply the ellipsis." Never mind that citizenship of a State is not the same as that of the United States, that to substitute one for the other is to rewrite the Constitution and significantly to alter a citizen's rights. For, as was said in *United States v.*

---

supra text accompanying note 18.

[28] Supra text accompanying note 8.

[29] Globe 1285. Stevens regarded the citizenship provision as an "excellent amendment, long needed to settle conflicting decisions." Avins 237.

[30] Minor v. Happersett, 88 U.S. (21 Wall.) 162, 171, (1874).

[31] Curtis, Book 59. Bingham read Article IV (2) to the House. Avins 157. He considered his "ellipsis" to be the "self-evident" meaning of the Article. Curtis, Book 61. "Citizen of each State" does not, however, self-evidently mean "citizen of the United States."

Justice Miller stated that Article IV (2) did not "profess to control the

Cruikshank, "the rights of citizenship under one of these governments will be different from those that he will have under the other."[32]

As we have seen, Curtis originally conceded that it is "difficult to show that Republicans read the original privileges and immunities clause to require the States to obey the Bill of Rights."[33] By the time he came to write his book those difficulties had vanished. Now he could flatly state, "Most Republicans who spoke on the subject in 1866 believed that the states were already required to obey the Bill of Rights. . . . Even those who did not accept the unorthodox Republican doctrines could agree that the Bill of Rights were privileges and immunities of citizens of the United States that should be shielded from hostile state action."[34] That was not the view of Thaddeus Stevens, the Radical leader: "[T]he Constitution limits only the action of Congress and is not a limitation of the States."[35] Senator Trumbull called attention to the judicial constructions of Article IV (2), none of which alluded to the Bill of Rights.[36] Others

---

power of State governments over the rights of its own citizens." Its sole purpose was to require that the rights granted by a State to its "own citizens . . . the same, neither more nor less shall be the measure of the rights of citizens of other States within your jurisdiction." Slaughter-House Cases, 83 U.S. (16 Wall.) 36, 77 (1872). There were Radical Republicans, e.g., Higby, who read Article IV (2) literally, so that "a citizen of New York would have been treated as a citizen in the State of North Carolina." Curtis, Book 68.

[32] 92 U.S. 542, 549 (1875).

[33] Supra text accompanying note 2.

[34] Curtis, Book 91.

[35] Id. 97. Curtis states, "Several Republicans, of course, believed a constitutional amendment was required to correct Barron v. Baltimore." Id. 233 note 201. Stevens and Bingham were among them, infra text accompanying notes 47 and 48.

[36] Supra Chapter 3 text accompanying notes 8–14.

were sadly confused.[37] The disparate Republican views make the legislative history invoked by Curtis inconclusive.

Curtis has yet to reconcile his expansive reading of "privileges or immunities" with Bingham's insistence that "civil rights or immunities" be deleted from the Civil Rights Bill because the terms were "oppressive" and would "strike down" State constitutions.[38] If notwithstanding, Bingham could fantasize about the Bill of Rights in reliance on the "immortal [and irrelevant] words" of Daniel Webster, the fact remains that the House, unmoved by Bingham's fantasy, *voted* to delete the "oppressive" words. It cannot reasonably be assumed that the House silently reversed itself by adopting "privileges or immunities." Curtis himself says of an early draft of the amendment "which prohibited discrimination in civil rights" that "Its general language failed to take account of and overrule the doctrine of *Barron v. Baltimore* that the Bill of Rights did not limit the States."[39] "Privileges or immunities" is no less general than "discrimination in civil rights" and equally would not overrule *Barron*. It is reasonable to conclude that the Framers adopted "privileges or immunities" precisely because the phrase, being of settled meaning, was not subject to the "oppressive" objection. The lawyers addressed by Senator Trumbull would readily understand the cases he quoted, holding, as William Lawrence later said, that "privileges or immunities" only applied to "some," not to all, privileges.[40] By a glance at

[37] Hiram Price understood the "intention" of the Amendment "is to give the same rights, privileges, and protection to the citizens of one State going to another that a citizen of that State would have who had lived there for years." Avins 156. Such protection for migrants was already provided by Article IV (2).

[38] Supra Chapter 2 text accompanying notes 29–31.

[39] Curtis, Book 84.

[40] Supra text accompanying note 9.

the Constitution they could easily perceive that the "privileges or immunities" of Article IV did not embrace the as yet unborn Bill of Rights. Whatever the "unorthodox beliefs" of diverse Republicans—so tirelessly recapitulated by Curtis—they cannot without more overcome Congress' adoption of the technical terms "privileges or immunities" which the Framers could perceive, and in fact were given to understand, were of limited scope.

A less expansive, non-"oppressive" construction would be better attuned to their attachment to State control of their own civil and criminal administration. Such considerations elicit no comment from Curtis. Referring to my "attribut[ion] to the Republicans [of] an unorthodox reading" of Article IV (2)—in fact, the attribution is his own[41]—he concludes that "Any attempt to define the Fourteenth Amendment's privileges or immunities clause by a rule of construction that gives it the *orthodox* content of the privileges and immunities of Article IV is not legitimate" because it defeats the "intention of the framers."[42] But he has failed to demonstrate that the "rankly heretical" views of some Republican radicals convinced the moderate-conservative majority who were told by Trumbull that the words had a "settled" meaning. To the contrary, Senator Sherman boasted that "we defeated every radical proposition."[43] Against this Bingham's "understanding" of Article IV (2) is not "of crucial importance."[44]

Before long Bingham himself was to recognize that the "privileges or immunities" of the Fourteenth Amendment were no greater than those of Article IV. On January 30,

[41] Curtis, Book 116; infra text accompanying note 46.
[42] Curtis, Book 116.
[43] James 167.
[44] Curtis, Book 59.

1871, he submitted a Report of the House Committee on the Judiciary, reciting:

> The clause of the fourteenth amendment "No State shall make or enforce any law which shall abridge the privileges or immunities of citizens of the United States," does not, in the opinion of the committee, refer to the privileges and immunities of citizens of the United States other than the privileges and immunities embraced in the original text of the Constitution, article 4, section 2. The fourteenth amendment, it is believed, *did not add* to the privileges or immunities before mentioned, but was deemed necessary for their enforcement as an express limitation upon the power of the States.[45]

There were two dissenters from the Report; Bingham was not one of them. In light of his prior reliance on that "immortal man, who sleeps alone in his honored tomb beside the sounding sea," for locating the Bill of Rights in Article IV, it is highly interesting that the Report quotes Daniel Webster's emphasis that Article IV put it beyond the power of any State to hinder entry "for the purposes of trade, commerce, buying and selling." Lawyer that he was, Webster well knew the judicial constructions limiting the clause.

It is time to examine more closely Curtis' reliance on the erroneous "beliefs" of some, not all, Republicans, that, for example, *Barron v. Baltimore* was wrongly decided, that the Article IV (2) "citizen of each State" language really meant "citizen of the United States." Some Republicans, Curtis acknowledges, "frankly recognized that their constitutional views were unorthodox." "Republicans," he states, "operated from unorthodox legal premises."[46] All the wishful thinking in the world cannot convert what *is* into what ought to be. Stevens put the matter in proper focus: "The Consti-

---

[45] Avins 466 (emphasis added).
[46] Curtis, Book 52, 113.

tution [including the Bill of Rights] limits only the action of Congress and is not a limitation on the States. This amendment *supplies that defect.*"[47] "Beliefs" could not cure the "defect." For that an amendment was needed, as Bingham recognized: "Bingham explicitly noted the case of *Barron v. Baltimore* to show why his *amendment was required.*"[48] Curtis notices three explicit amendments. Republicans

> rejected *Dred Scott* and instead believed that all free persons born in the United States were citizens of the United States. Still, they *explicitly wrote into* the Fourteenth Amendment national citizenship for all persons born in the United States. Some believed, contrary to *Barron v. Baltimore*, that the states could not deprive persons of due process. Still, they *wrote this limitation into* the Fourteenth Amendment. Finally, leading Republicans believed that no state could abridge the privileges and immunities of citizens of the United States—including those privileges secured by the Bill of Rights. This idea also *was written into* [?] the Fourteenth Amendment.[49]

From this Curtis infers that "for Republicans the amendment was simply *declaratory* of existing constitutional law, properly understood."[50] This represents yet another erroneous "belief." A declaratory statute "declare[s] what the law is and ever had been" in order to remove "doubts."[51] "What the law is" was stated by *Barron v. Baltimore* and was subsisting law in 1866. A declaratory act would confirm, not

---

[47] Id. 86. Senator Howard, who with Bingham is one of the two pillars of Curtis' case, stated that the first eight amendments "do not operate in the slightest degree as a restraint or prohibition upon State legislation. States are not affected by them." Avins 219.

[48] Id. 101 (emphasis added). See supra Chapter 6 note 99.

[49] Id. 91 (emphasis added).

[50] Id. (emphasis added).

[51] 1 William Blackstone, *Commentaries on the Laws of England* 86 (1765–1769).

overrule, it. Radical abolitionist repudiation of *Barron* did not give rise to the "doubt" which a declaratory statute would dispel.[52]

Curtis' three examples demonstrate that the framers well knew how to articulate *their* aims. Curtis notes that the amendment "was rewritten to incorporate this understanding [citizens of the United States] *explicitly*."[53] Aware of the significance of the framers' resort to "explicit" provisions, Curtis states,

> One could ask why "the Bill of Rights" was not explicitly written into the Fourteenth Amendment, as due process and citizenship were. The reason, of course, is that the rights in the Bill of Rights make up the most important, but not all, of the rights of a citizen of the United States.[54]

By this reasoning, a failure explicitly to provide justifies an interpolation going far beyond the express provision. By this twisted logic, express provision for due process was unnecessary because omission of the Bill of Rights testifies to an intention to comprehend *all* its rights.[55] That inference is confuted by the record. First, Bingham vehemently protested against the "oppressive" breadth of the words "civil rights," which thereupon were deleted in order to foreclose an "unintended latitudinarian" construction. Second, time and again the framers rejected motions to prohibit *all* discriminations.[56] One such proposal had been made by Stevens; in the end he pleaded for the amendment, though lamenting, as did Senator Fessenden, that it did not go far

[52] Curtis, Book 42, 48, 121.
[53] Id. 115 (emphasis added).
[54] Id. 125 (emphasis added).
[55] "An omission of the words implie[s] an omission of the purpose." Pirie v. Chicago Title & Trust Co., 182 U.S. 438, 448 (1901).
[56] For citations, see Berger, *Judiciary* 163.

enough but represented the most that the people would accept.[57] To turn a blind eye to such undeniable facts, to resort instead to strained speculation and distortion, to dismiss what leading spokesmen said because to his eyes it seems "very odd" renders Curtis' scholarship suspect.[58]

In a decision contemporaneous with the Fourteenth Amendment, respecting the First Amendment right to assemble, Chief Justice Waite declared,

> This . . . was not intended to limit the powers of the State government . . . but to operate upon the National government alone. For their protection in its enjoyment, therefore, the people must look to the State. The power for that purpose was originally placed there, and it *has never been surrendered* to the United States.[59]

Waite cannot very well be taxed with ignorance of the Fourteenth Amendment. To the contrary, as Justice William Johnson earlier observed, contemporaries "had the best opportunity of informing themselves of the understanding of the framers . . . and of the sense put upon it by the people when it was adopted by them."[60] Justice Black's "discovery" that the Amendment incorporated the Bill of Rights had to wait for almost eighty years, and then only to be consistently rejected by his Bretheren.

---

[57] Benjamin Kendrick, *The Journal of the Joint Committee of Fifteen on Reconstruction* 46 (1914). Globe 3148, 705, quoted infra Conclusion text accompanying notes 1–3.

[58] Yet Curtis has the temerity to declare that "Professor Fairman's treatment of the amendment lacked balance." Curtis, Book 109. "History for the activist is a protean instrument, useful for legitimating a predetermined result." L. Levy, *Judgments: Essays in American Constitutional History* 78 (1972).

[59] United States v. Cruikshank, 92 U.S. 542, 552 (1875) (emphasis added).

[60] Ogden v. Saunders, 25 U.S. (12 Wheat.) 212, 290 (1827).

CHAPTER EIGHT

"Fundamental" and "Absolute" Rights

"FUNDAMENTAL" RIGHTS

CURTIS rings the changes on "fundamental rights," jumping off from *Corfield*'s reference thereto, and quoting Trumbull's "'Citizens of the United States' have 'fundamental rights—*such as* the rights enumerated in this bill'."[1] "Such as" is not illustrative of a larger class but indicates that the subsequent enumeration determines the meaning of "fundamental rights."[2] Moreover, Trumbull observed that *Corfield* enumerates "*the very rights* belonging to a citizen of the United States which are *set forth* in the first section of the bill."[3] Thus the Bill specified the fundamental rights, and howsoever *Corfield* may be read, the subsequent Bill is the higher authority. Curtis also quotes from Trumbull's criticism of President Johnson's veto of the Bill: "[E]ach State, *so that it does not abridge the great fundamental rights belonging under the Constitution to all citizens*, may

---

[1] Curtis, Book 114.

[2] See *Oxford Universal Dictionary*, "such" II.

[3] Avins 122 (emphasis added). This statement carried weight with Justice Field. *Corfield*, he stated, "was cited by Senator Trumbull with the observation that it enumerated the very rights belonging to a citizen of the United States set forth in the first section of the Act . . . that these were the great fundamental rights set forth in the act." Slaughter-House Cases, 83 U.S. (16 Wall.) 36, 98 (1872). Field and his fellow dissenters read the privileges and immunities phrase more broadly than did the majority.

grant or withhold such rights as it pleases." (Emphasis in original.) From this he deduces, "Clearly in 1866 Trumbull had in mind some absolute rights seen as belonging to citizens under the Constitution."[4] Trumbull was concerned with a particular right—"privileges and immunities"—and with its scope. This he tied to specifics:

> The *great fundamental rights set forth in the bill:* the right to acquire property, the right to come and go at pleasure, the right to enforce rights in the courts, to make contracts, and to inherit and dispose of property. *These are the very rights* that are set forth in this bill as pertaining to every freeman.

This was his answer to the question what are the rights of citizens.[5] "One might rely on this quotation," Curtis says, to prove that there was not room left in the privileges and immunities clause of the Fourteenth Amendment for the Bill of Rights liberties."[6] But he disparages this in reliance on Trumbull's above-quoted criticism of President Johnson's veto. Curtis forgets that the specific governs the general,[7] that Trumbull's hearers would not infer that he was attempting to enlarge the specific enumerations of the Bill by implications drawn from what he allegedly "had in mind . . . some absolute rights."

Such inferences must also account for Martin Thayer's

[4] Curtis, Book 117. Curtis regards the italicized remarks as "more precise" than Trumbull's explicit enumeration. Id. 73.

[5] Avins 122 (emphasis added). Such facts undermine Curtis' reliance on Fairman's "conce[ssion] that the reference to fundamental rights in Corfield 'cloud[s]' the simple antidiscrimination reading of Article IV, section 2, that he advocated." Curtis, Book 115.

[6] Curtis, Book 117.

[7] Ginsberg & Sons v. Popkin, 285 U.S. 204, 208 (1932); Fourco Glass Co. v. Transmirra Products Corp., 353 U.S. 222 (1957). The rule is of long standing; "Where a Thing is given or limited by particular Words in a Statute, this shall not be taken away or altered by any subsequent general

parallel explanation to the House: "to avoid any misapprehension" as to what the "fundamental rights of citizenship" are, *they are stated in the bill. The same section goes on to define with greater particularity the civil rights and immunities which are protected by the bill." And he added, "when those civil rights which are first referred to in general terms in the bill are subsequently enumerated, that enumeration *precludes any possibility* that the general words which have been used *can be extended beyond the particulars* which have been enumerated," and that the Bill was for "the protection of the fundamental rights [thus enumerated] of citizenship and *nothing else.*"[8] What could more precisely bar resort to generalities for expansion "beyond the particulars"? Such assurances were calculated to allay fear of undue encroachment on the States' sphere.[9]

Even a Radical, William Windom,[10] said that under the Civil Rights Bill, blacks

----

words." 4 Matthew Bacon, *A New Abridgement of the Law,* "Statutes," section 2, p. 645 (1759). See Curtis' concession, supra Chapter 2 note 32.

[8] Avins 169. Thayer echoed the maxim *expressio unius est exclusio alterius.* See supra chapter 6 note 43.

Curtis would distinguish Thayer's remarks on the ground that he merely denied that the bill included the right to vote. Curtis, Book 79. As Wilson made plain, it is not necessary to mention every item that is not included. More significant is Thayer's statement that "The amendment incorporat[ed] in the Constitution . . . the principle of the civil rights bill which has lately become a law . . . in order that [it] . . . shall be forever incorporated in the Constitution." Curtis, Book 86.

Samuel Shellabarger, addressing a bill in 1869 to secure the "privileges or immunities" of the Fourteenth Amendment, referred to the "well known and universally recognized principle of law, expressio unius exclusio alterius." Avins 347. See supra Chapter 6 note 43.

[9] See Judge Posner, supra Chapter 1 note 55; see also supra Chapter 5 text accompanying notes 24–31.

[10] Curtis, Book 89.

shall have an equal right, *nothing more* . . . to make and enforce contracts, to give evidence in court, and to hold and enjoy real and personal property. . . . It merely provides safeguards to shield them from wrong and outrage, and to protect them in the enjoyment of that lowest right of human nature, the right to exist. *Its object is* to secure to a poor, weak class of laborers the right to make contracts for their labor, the power to enforce the payment of their wages, and the means of holding and enjoying the proceeds of their toil.[11]

Emphasis on generalities in place of the limiting particulars sets at naught the framers' carefully drawn purposes. As Senator Sherman stated, the bill

defines what are the incidents of freedom, and says that these men must be protected in certain rights, and so careful is its language that it goes on to define those rights, the right to sue and be sued, to plead and be impleaded, to acquire and hold property, and other universal incidents of freedom.[12]

Curtis concedes that "Although many Republicans believed that 'fundamental' rights not explicitly listed in the Constitution, were included, there *was no consensus* on what these rights were."[13] The absence of a "consensus" vitiates the attempt to forge legislative history from disparate utterances. Curtis also observes that "Much of what Republicans had to say "*does seem confused* if read without understanding the antislavery background and *in light of modern legal ideas*."[14] It is a historical fallacy to impose "upon the past a creature of our own imagining."[15] "One must be on his guard," wrote Felix Frankfurter, "against attributing to language of an early legal doctrine the implications which the

[11] Avins 171 (emphasis added).

[12] Id. 144.

[13] Curtis, Book 82 (emphasis added).

[14] Id. 100 (emphasis added).

[15] H. Richardson & G. Sayles, "Parliament and Great Councils in Medieval England," 77 L.Q. Rev. 213, 224 (1961).

evolution of experience has put into it,"[16] a caution earlier sounded by Justice Iredell.[17] Curtis himself recognizes that "Of course, it is anachronistic to see the Republican understanding of rights essential to freedom in light of fashionable modern ideas."[18] And as we have seen, in seeking to filter antislavery ideology into the thinking of the majority of the framers, Curtis is wildly off course.[19]

Behind the utterances of Trumbull, Sherman, et al., was reluctance to expand "rights" unduly lest they encroach on a State's control over its own internal affairs, as Trumbull's criticism of President Johnson's veto makes clear:

> This bill in no manner interferes with the municipal regulations of any State which protects all alike in their rights of person and property. It could have no operation in Massachusetts, New York, Illinois or most of the States in the Union.[20]

This reflects the framers' devotion to State sovereignty.[21] State control of local institutions, Phillip Paludan repeat-

---

[16] Felix Frankfurter, *The Commerce Clause Under Marshall, Taney and Waite* 60 (1937).

[17] "We are too apt, in estimating a law passed at a remote period, to combine in our consideration, all the subsequent events which have had an influence upon it, instead of confining ourselves (which we ought to do) to the existing circumstances at the time of its passing." Ware v. Hylton, 3 U.S. (3 Dall.) 199, 267 (1796). In "the construction of the language of the Constitution . . . we are to place ourselves as nearly as possible in the condition of the men who framed the instrument." *Ex parte* Bain, 112 U.S. 1, 12 (1887). Walton Hamilton & Douglas Adair, *The Power to Govern* 104 (1937): "It is the importation of meaning, opinion, and the intellectual world of here and now which makes evidence inconclusive, muddles understanding, and shunts inquiry to false leads."

[18] Curtis, Book 67.

[19] Supra Chapter 5 text accompanying notes 47–101.

[20] Avins 200. The impact of the Bill and the Amendment on the North was largely downplayed; attention was focussed on Southern misdeeds. Supra Chapter 4 text accompanying notes 7–15.

[21] Supra Chapter 5 text accompanying notes 23–45.

edly emphasized, was "the most potent institutional obstacle to the Negroes' hope for protected liberty."[22] Wilson assured the House that "If the States would all practice the constitutional declaration" of Article IV and enforce it we might very well refrain from the enactment of this bill into a law."[23] Plainly the Bill did not postulate an indeterminate catalog of "absolute rights." Its face shows that it struck at discrimination with respect to enumerated particulars. The "entire structure of this bill," said Wilson, "rests on the discrimination . . . on account of race."[24]

Not content with the framers' own specification of "fundamental rights," Curtis ransacks Blackstone. Wilson had cited Blackstone to explain the "great fundamental civil rights" to the House, saying, "Blackstone classifies them under three articles as follows:

1. The right of personal security; which, he says, 'Consists in a person's legal and uninterrupted enjoyment of his life, his limbs, his body, his health and his reputation.'

2. The right of personal liberty; and this, he says, 'Consists in the power of locomotion, of changing situation, or moving one's person to what ever place one's inclination may direct, without impairment or restraint, unless by the course of law.'

3. The right of personal property; which he defines to be 'The free use and enjoyment, and disposal of all his acquisitions, without any control or diminution save only the laws of the land'."[25]

[22] Phillip Paludan, *A Covenant With Death* 15, 13, 51, 54 (1975). See also H. Hyman, *A More Perfect Union* 470 (1973).

[23] Avins 163–64. The derivation of the Bill from Article IV is constantly to be borne in mind. Chairman Trumbull explained that it had been patterned on the privileges and immunities of Article IV (2). Avins 122–23.

[24] Id. 164.

[25] Curtis, Book 74–75. For "locomotion" see supra Chapter 2 text accompanying notes 22–24; supra Chapter 6 text accompanying note 77.

These rights were expressed in the "life, liberty and property" of the due process clause, terms which had a down-to-earth meaning for the framers. The life of the emancipated black was being threatened and often taken in the South;[26] consequently the Civil Rights Bill guaranteed "security of person and property," and the framers frequently used those terms,[27] explaining, as did Windom, in order "to shield them from wrong and outrage."[28] They employed the particulars of the bill, Shellabarger explained, because those rights were "necessary" for the "protection of the rights of person and property."[29] Wilson himself, referring to the due process protection of life, liberty, and property, told the House, "I understand that these constitute the civil rights . . . to which the bill relates."[30] Blackstone's definition of "'liberty' as the power of locomotion," of moving freely from place to place, snugly met the Black Codes' attempts to fetter the freedmen. Senator Henry Wilson urged the framers to ensure that the freedman "can go where he pleases."[31] The Civil Rights Bill, Trumbull explained, secures "the right to go and come at pleasure."[32] During the Ratification campaign it was stressed that the Bill secured the right "to be protected in their person and property, the

[26] Wilson stated, "Thousands and tens of thousands of harmless black men . . . have been wronged and outraged by violence, and hundreds upon hundreds have been murdered." Avins 171. And see supra Chapter 4 note 9.

[27] Curtis, Book 77, 78, 79.

[28] Supra text accompanying note 11. James Wilson referred to "Laws barbaric and treatment inhuman." Avins 164. See also supra Chapter 2 note 19, Chapter 6 note 63.

[29] Supra Chapter 6 text accompanying note 55.

[30] Avins 189.

[31] Supra Chapter 2 text accompanying note 24.

[32] Avins 122; see also James Wilson, supra Chapter 2 text accompanying note 24.

right of locomotion—the right to go where they please."[33] All that was involved, to quote Chancellor Kent, as did Wilson, was "the right of personal security, the right of personal liberty, and the right to acquire and enjoy property."[34] So there was no occasion to invest "life, liberty and property" with unplumbed depths.

Not satisfied with such mundane explanations, Curtis searches Blackstone and emerges with references to "Magna Charta, the Petition of Right, the Habeas Corpus Act, the English Bill of Rights, and Act of Settlement"[35]—the last, governing succession to the throne, is altogether irrelevant to our Republic. In Federalist No. 84, Hamilton said that Magna Charta and the Bill of Rights "have no application to constitutions, professedly founded upon the power of the people."[36] True, the Bill of Rights was soon added to the Constitution; but of what use was it to specify rights in the Bill if the enumeration was expansible by mere reference to Blackstone? If more than those specifications was involved, the framers were entitled to be told. And what relevance does Blackstone's reference to the Bill of Rights have in light of *Barron v. Baltimore*'s ruling that our own Bill of Rights does not apply to the States? Consider Magna Charta; it requires trial by jury of one's peers, but the framers of the Fourteenth Amendment were assured that blacks could not serve as jurors.[37] Certainly Wilson, who read Blackstone to the House, did not take Curtis' untrammeled view; he explained that "Civil rights and immunities" did not mean that

[33] Bond 448.
[34] Avins 164.
[35] Curtis, Book 75.
[36] The Federalist, No. 84 at 558 (Mod. Lib. ed. 1937).
[37] Berger, Judiciary 163; infra text accompanying note 59.

in all things civil, social and political, all citizens, without distinction of race or color shall be equal. . . . Nor do they mean that all citizens shall sit on juries, or that their children shall attend the same schools. . . . I understand civil rights to be simply the absolute rights of individuals, such as "The right of personal security, the right of personal liberty, and the right to acquire and enjoy property."[38]

These had been defined by the Blackstone excerpt he quoted. And he rejected a construction that the Bill "invades the States . . . in respect to those things which properly and rightfully depend on State regulations and laws," instancing "school laws and jury laws."[39] Wilson, wrote Alfred Kelly, an activist, "declared for a narrow interpretation of the measure in unequivocal terms."[40] In his own pioneer study of the Fourteenth Amendment's history, Alexander Bickel commented, "Wilson thus presented the Civil Rights Bill to the House as a measure of limited and definite objectives. In this he followed the lead of the majority in the Senate. . . . And the line he laid down was followed by others who spoke for the Bill in the House."[41]

"ABSOLUTE" RIGHTS

In comparing the Civil Rights Bill and the Fourteenth Amendment, Curtis addresses the "argument" that

the Civil Rights Bill was merely designed to protect blacks by granting them equal protection in certain narrow rights secured by state law—the right to contract, own property, and the like. The Fourteenth Amendment, in turn, merely incor-

[38] Avins 163, quoting Kent's Commentaries.
[39] Avins 189.
[40] Alfred Kelly, "The Fourteenth Amendment Reconsidered: The Segregation Question," 54 Mich. L. Rev. 1049, 1066 (1965).
[41] Bickel 17.

porated the Civil Rights Bill read narrowly. The whole object, according to this view, was to grant certain rights to blacks—basically, the rights to contract, sell, testify, and to equal protection of certain state laws.[42]

It is Curtis' depressing habit to label as "argument" that which is indisputable. Disparagement of "narrow rights" "read narrowly" conflicts with the Court's statement that "The legislative history of the 1866 act clearly indicates that Congress intended to protect a *limited category* of rights,"[43] as the evidence herein detailed confirms.

He goes on to comment,

> The argument claims that the Fourteenth Amendment is absolutely the same as the Civil Rights Bill. Since the "act was merely to secure blacks against discrimination and not to displace nondiscriminatory state law," by this view the Fourteenth Amendment does not protect Bill of Rights' liberties or any other absolute rights that states cannot abridge.[44]

For this Curtis cites my discussion of the *Act* wherein I considered his argument that if "the amendment and the bill were identical it follows that the Civil Rights Bill contained a *federal* standard of due process," observing that "Since the object of the Act merely was to secure blacks against discrimination, not to displace undiscriminatory State law, that interpretation meant the standard of the State."[45] No reference was made by me to the Amendment. The focus of my *Government by Judiciary*, it needs to be borne in mind, was on the *substantive* rights enumerated in the Civil Rights Bill; those rights were to be free of discrimination and included access to the courts for their protection. The

---

[42] Curtis, Book 118.
[43] Supra Chapter 2 text accompanying note 32.
[44] Curtis, Book 118, 119.
[45] Id. 247 notes 194–95, Berger, "*Reply*" 4–5.

Amendment tersely articulated the purposes of the Bill in the several clauses. I would not urge that "identical" means "absolutely the same" in every particular. There *was* a difference between Act and Amendment, as Stevens pointed out—the Amendment could not be repealed by a subsequent Congress.[46] Curtis' reliance on legislative history is incompatible with making a fortress out of the dictionary.

Let us recur to Curtis' argument that to read the Amendment "to prohibit discrimination in certain rights that states choose to accord their own citizens" renders the privileges or immunities and due process clauses "superfluous."[47] This argument is built on Curtis' strait-jacket understanding of the word "identical." Since we are analyzing an historical relation, it will be useful to begin with the Civil Rights Bill.

THE CIVIL RIGHTS BILL

Unquestionably, the Bill was aimed at racial discrimination: "there shall be no discrimination in civil rights or immunities . . . on account of race."[48] Although this clause was deleted in deference to Bingham's protest against its "oppressive" invasion of the States' domain, the antidiscriminatory essence of the Bill remained in the Act's provision that all citizens born in the United States "shall have the same right . . . to make and enforce contracts, to sue [etc.] . . . [as is enjoyed by white citizens]."[49] Senator Trumbull, Manager of the Bill, explained that it "will have no operation in

[46] Supra Chapter 6 text accompanying note 2.
[47] Curtis, Book 119, quoted supra Chapter 6 at note 5.
[48] Supra Chapter 2 text accompanying note 26.
[49] Id.; Avins 243. Wilson emphasized that "A colored citizen shall not, because he is colored, be subjected to obligations, duties, pains and penalties from which others are exempted," in short "equality in the exemptions of the law." Id. 163. See also Wilson, infra text accompanying note 59.

any State where the laws are equal, where all persons have the same civil rights without regard to color or race."[50] After the Bill was vetoed by President Andrew Johnson, Trumbull assured the framers that it "in no manner interferes with . . . any State which protects all alike in their rights of person or property."[51] Similarly, Samuel Shellabarger stated, "whatever rights as to each of these enumerated civil (not political) matters the State may *confer* upon one race . . . shall be held by all races in equality. . . . It secures . . . *equality of protection* in those *enumerated civil rights* which the States *may deem proper to confer* upon any one race."[52] Martin Thayer emphasized that the enumeration of rights in the bill "precludes any possibility that the general words which have been used can be extended beyond the particulars which have been enumerated."[53] Plainly, the Act did not "displace nondiscriminatory State law"; it only required that if whites were given certain rights by States they must also be enjoyed by blacks. Even so limited, the Bill, Bingham protested, constituted an "oppressive" invasion of the States' domain; hence, the words "civil rights" were deleted in order to foreclose an unintended "latitudinarian construction."[54]

Curtis asserts that the "ban on discrimination collides with . . . the absolute rights of 'personal security,' 'personal liberty,' and 'the right to acquire and enjoy property'."[55] He relies on remarks, labeling them as "inalienable," "absolute rights . . . of which a State cannot deprive him," and argues

[50] Id. 122.

[51] Id. 200.

[52] Id. 188 (emphasis added). Curtis regards these remarks as "qualified and ambiguous"! Curtis, Book 78. This from one who tortures every utterance to find a place for the Bill of Rights.

[53] Supra Chapter 2 text accompanying note 28.

[54] Id. text accompanying notes 29–32.

[55] Curtis, Book 119.

that "If the States could eliminate such rights so long as they did it for all their citizens, the rights would not be inalienable."[56] Curtis' reliance on Trumbull lends him no aid: "Trumbull noted in arguing for the Civil Rights Bill, the rights to personal liberty, personal security, and the right to acquire property 'are declared to be inalienable rights'."[57] Nevertheless, as has been noted, Trumbull stated that the Bill "will have no operation where . . . all persons have the same civil rights without regard to color or race," that it "in no manner interferes with . . . any State which protects all alike."[58] Clearly Trumbull was only concerned with discrimination, leaving the States free to withhold or repeal laws conferring rights. Nor does another such citation to Wilson advance Curtis' case. Wilson, House manager for the Bill, observed that the "entire structure of this bill rests on the discrimination . . . on account of race."[59] He also stated that had the Southern States complied with Article IV, the Bill would have been "unnecessary."[60] And he assured the Framers that the Bill did not mean that "in all things, civil, social and political, all citizens without distinction of race or color shall be equal."[61]

There remains Curtis' citation to William Lawrence: "there are certain absolute rights . . . which are inherent, and of which a state cannot constitutionally deprive" a citizen.[62] And he stated that citizens "may not be stripped by

---

[56] Id.

[57] Id. During the Ratification campaign Trumbull declared that section 1 of the Amendment was "a reiteration of the rights as set forth in the Civil Rights Bill." Supra Chapter 4 note 17.

[58] Avins 122, and supra text accompanying note 51.

[59] Avins 164.

[60] Id. 163–64.

[61] Id. 163.

[62] Curtis, Book 119.

State authority of the means by which citizens may exist"; [63] but this was against the background of Southern denial of those rights to blacks alone. He amplified:

> It is idle to say that a citizen shall have the right to life, and yet deny him the right to labor, whereby alone he can live. It is a mockery to say that a citizen may have a right to live, and yet deny him the right to make a contract to secure the privileges and rewards of his labor. [64]

The very spelling out in the Civil Rights Act of rights that were to be free from *discrimination* precludes an attribution to the framers of a doctrine of "absolute" rights that were beyond State power to withdraw them from *all*. To the contrary, the assurances by Trumbull, Shellabarger, Thayer, and Wilson that when States granted certain rights they had to be available to all indicates that whether to grant or withdraw them was left in the States' discretion, a far cry from "inalienable" rights.

Curtis' unceasing drumbeat on "personal liberty," "personal security," invests them with near mystical significance. The framers, however, viewed them concretely—protecting the emancipated blacks from "laws barbaric and treatment inhuman," from "crimes and outrages," murder and torture. [65] If "personal liberty," "personal security" range further, beyond the rights particularized in the Bill, the framers were guilty of an egregious oversight. Vain was their effort to limit protection to the enumerated particulars of the Bill. What need was there for particularization if there existed a galaxy of "absolute rights" outside its confines? For the framers, however, as Thayer stated, "the fundamental rights

---

[63] Avins 206. But compare Shellabarger, supra Chapter 6 text accompanying note 17.

[64] Avins 206.

[65] Id. 164, 472; see also supra Chapter 4 note 9.

of citizens . . . are stated in the Bill."[66] Senator Trumbull likewise referred to "[t]he great fundamental rights set forth in the bill."[67] As to these, there could be no discrimination. It is open to Curtis to insist that the Civil Rights Act was and remains fatally defective both because it does not guard against State repeal of the rights the Bill enumerates, and because "absolute rights" embrace still others. But he may not saddle the framers with his view.

THE FOURTEENTH AMENDMENT

The "privileges or immunities" clause, it will be recalled, was the "primary source of substantive protection"; as Curtis put it, "it played the central role."[68] Drawn from Article IV (2), which protected rights associated with "trade and commerce," it protected a "limited category" of rights, without which the freedman could not exist.[69] Michael Perry concluded that by "privileges or immunities" the framers

> meant only to protect, against state discrimination on the basis of race, a narrow category of "fundamental" rights: those pertaining to the physical security of one's person, freedom of movement, and capacity to make contracts . . . and to acquire,

[66] Supra Chapter 2 text accompanying note 28.

[67] Avins 122. Notwithstanding, Gressman opines that "Citing chapter and verse from the legislative history, Curtis concludes that the framers clearly intended to incorporate into the Privileges and Immunities clause all the rights expressed in the Bill of Rights, plus all the other rights that might be deemed fundamental to a free people." Gressman, "Book Review," 1 New Law Books Reviewer 57, 59–60 (1986). He concludes that "Curtis's book made clear beyond all doubt that the framers . . . did intend to incorporate an open-ended definition of all other fundamental rights that 'belong, of right, to the citizens of all free governments'." Id. 62. An activist's eagerness to believe blurs judgment.

[68] Supra Chapter 1 text accompanying note 1; Curtis, Book 9.

[69] Supra Chapter 2 text accompanying note 32.

hold and transfer chattels and land—"life, liberty, and property" in the original sense.[70]

The right to sue for the protection of those rights was embodied in the due process clause, which had a centuries-old procedural connotation.[71]

EQUAL PROTECTION OF THE LAWS

"Equal protection of the laws" restated affirmatively the Act's negatively framed proscription of discrimination. Stevens explained that the Amendment "allows Congress to correct the unjust legislation of the States, *so far* that the law which operates upon one man shall operate equally upon all. Whatever law punishes a white man for a crime shall punish the black man precisely in the same way. . . . I need not enumerate those partial and oppressive laws,"[72] i.e., the Black Codes. This was made explicit by Leonard Myers who, in commenting on the Amendment, observed that a "change" was required so that "each State shall provide for equality before the law, *equal protection* to life, liberty and property, equal right to sue and be sued, to inherit, make contracts, and give testimony,"[73] wedding "equal protection" to the components of the Civil Rights Bill.

Curtis does not explicitly invoke the equal protection clause as an independent source of substantive rights, but

[70] Michael Perry, "Interpretivism, Freedom of Expression and Equal Protection," 42 Ohio St. L.J. 261, 273 (1981). Shellabarger referred to "those rights to contract, sue, testify, inherit &c., which this bill says the races shall hold as races in equality, are of that class which are fairly conductive and necessary as means to the constitutional end, to wit, the protection of the rights of person and property of a citizen." Avins 188.

[71] See supra Chapter 1 text accompanying notes 20–22. See also Edward Corwin, *The Twilight of the Supreme Court* 95 (1934).

[72] Avins 212 (emphasis added).

[73] Id. 193 (emphasis added).

refers to Lincoln's reference during a campaign to the statement in the Declaration of Independence that "all men [are]
created equal—equal in 'certain inalienable rights, among
which are life, liberty and the pursuit of happiness'."[74] But
as President, Lincoln told a delegation of black leaders that
"you are far removed from being placed on an equality with
the white man."[75] Equal protection was not an expression
of boundless equality, for the framers repeatedly rejected
proposals to ban *all* discrimination.[76] Plainly it did not comprehend suffrage.[77] "One is driven by the evidence," wrote
C. Vann Woodward, "to the conclusion . . . that popular
convictions were not prepared to sustain" "a guarantee of

[74] Curtis, Book 16.
[75] Supra Chapter 5 text accompanying note 58. In an 1859 campaign
speech, Lincoln said,

> I have no purpose to introduce political and social equality between
> the white and black races. There is a physical difference between the
> two which, in my judgment, will probably forbid their ever living to-
> gether upon the footing of perfect equality, and inasmuch as it be-
> comes necessary that there must be a difference, I, as well as Judge
> Douglas, am in favor of the race to which I belong having the superior
> position.

In his Columbus, Ohio, speech in September 1859, he quoted from an earlier address: "I am not or ever have been in favor of making voters or
jurors of negroes, nor of qualifying them to hold office or to intermarry
with the white people." Quoted Avins 242–43. Such remarks attest to an
electorate that was stirred by the very fears Lincoln sought to allay.
[76] For citations, see Berger, *Judiciary* 163.
[77] Commenting on §2 of the Fourteenth Amendment, which reduces
representation in the House of Representatives in proportion as a State
denies the franchise to blacks, Senator Jacob Howard commented,

> This section of the amendment does not recognize the authority of the
> United States over the question of suffrage in the several States at all;
> nor does it recognize, much less secure, the right of suffrage to the
> colored race. . . . [T]hree fourths of the States of the Union could not
> be induced to vote to grant the right of suffrage, even in any degree or

equality."[78] An Illinois Radical, John Farnsworth, asserted in the Thirty-ninth Congress that "Negro equality is the everlasting skeleton which frightens some people."[79] A black academician, Derrick Bell, has noted that "few abolitionists were interested in offering blacks the equality they touted so highly. Indeed the anguish most abolitionists experienced as to whether slaves should be granted social equality as well as political freedom is well documented."[80] David Donald, a Reconstruction historian, wrote, "[T]he suggestion that Negroes should be treated as equals to white men woke some of the deepest and ugliest fears in the American mind."[81] If we look to the legislative history—Curtis' springboard—equal protection cannot be given unbounded scope; it cannot be read to create substantive rights extending beyond those comprehended in the "privileges or immunities" clause. Nor does the text afford much comfort; John Hart Ely considers it to be "inscrutable."[82] The residuary jurisdiction guaranteed to the States by the Tenth Amendment cannot be curtailed under the cover of language lacking perceptible boundaries.[83]

What then is the substantive content of the words "equal protection of the laws"? The almost exclusive focus on

---

under any restrictions, to the colored race. . . . The second section leaves the right to regulate the elective franchise still with the States, and does not meddle with that right.

Avins 220. See Trumbull, supra Chapter 6 note 17.

[78] C. V. Woodward, *The Burden of Southern History* 83 (1960).

[79] Globe 204.

[80] Derrick Bell, "Book Review," 76 Colum. L. Rev. 350, 358 (1976).

[81] David Donald, *Charles Sumner and the Rights of Man* 157 (1970).

[82] "Like the inscrutable" privileges or immunities clause, the equal protection clause "is also unforthcoming with details." J. H. Ely, *Democracy and Distrust* 98 (1980).

[83] Supra Chapter 5 note 44.

"equal" has obscured the significance of the word "protection." Yet it is "protection" that is the subject of discourse; "equal" is the modifier. Whatever "protection" is furnished must be "equal." What, it needs to be asked, was to be protected? The abysmal failure of the South to protect the "person and property" of blacks against violence and murder, to safeguard the means whereby they could exist, furnishes the answer.[84] That approach can rescue analysis from treating the word "equal" as if it were a crystal ball. "Protection," if given, must be impartial.

The Bill leaves no doubt as to what was to be protected. Shellabarger explained that it secures "equality of protection *in those enumerated civil rights* which the States may deem proper to confer upon any races."[85] There was need, said Leonard Myers of the Amendment, to provide "equal protection to life, liberty, and property, equal right to sue and be sued, to inherit, make contracts, and give testimony."[86] Only when "equal protection" is viewed as a restatement of the Bill's ban on discrimination with respect to particular rights does it respond to the framers' intention. Neither the "privileges or immunities" nor the "due process" clauses address discrimination; that is the function of "equal protection." It does not follow that "due process" and "privileges or immunities" are "superfluous"; the latter describes the rights that are to be protected, and the "due process" clause affords them judicial protection.

Curtis threw his "superfluous" spotlight on the wrong clause. His argument led me to reexamine the relation between the three clauses, and it dawned on me that, if any, it may be the "equal protection" clause that is superfluous.

[84] Supra text accompanying notes 26–27.
[85] Avins 188 (emphasis added).
[86] Id. 193.

Discrimination is comprehended in the "privileges or immunities" phrase "No State shall . . . abridge"; for discrimination "abridges" the rights of the victim. Rights which may not be abridged stand in no need of "equal protection." The legislative history establishes that "equal protection" articulates the ban on discrimination respecting rights embodied in the "privileges or immunities" clause, and that it was not meant to be an independent source of substantive rights. The contrary view would render the central "privileges or immunities" clause supererogatory because the rights it incorporates would be comprehended in the boundless ambit of "equal protection." That view collides with the preponderant role "privileges or immunities" played in the debates.[87] How could the framers have overlooked this tautology? Originally the Bingham draft centered on equal protection; it did not contain the word "abridged." That word, Curtis recounts, appeared in Bingham's proposal of April 28, 1866.[88] Although I have read the three clauses countless times, I too have overlooked what now seems to me the duplication of "abridged" by "equal protection." This suggestion calls for further exploration.

In sum, the drive to preserve the Civil Rights Act from repeal, the derivation of the "privileges or immunities" clause from the Act, and the provision that "No State shall abridge the privileges or immunities" put it beyond the power of a State to curtail or withhold the rights the clause subsumes. By the same token, it lies beyond State power to "deprive any person of life, liberty, or property without due process of law," although that process is governed by State, not federal standards. In these respects the Amendment

[87] Curtis, Book 60–73, 78–80, 87–88, 90.
[88] Id. 57–58.

is not "absolutely the same" as the Civil Rights Act—it cannot be repealed by a subsequent Congress, and the rights it protects from abridgement cannot be withdrawn by a State from its citizens.

STATEWIDE EQUALITY

Curtis devotes a section of his book to "Equal National Rights or Equal Rights Within a State."[89] If, as seems to be the case, he questions Fairman's understanding of the Bill as "provid[ing] for equality under *state* or local law,"[90] he betrays unfamiliarity with the facts. It is hardly deniable that the equal protection clause referred to statewide, not national, "equality." At the outset Stevens had proposed that "all laws, state or *federal,* shall operate impartially and equally."[91] But his proposal came to naught. On the other hand, Trumbull spoke of "any State which shall protect all alike," Shellabarger of rights conferred by States, and Stevens of "correct[ing] the unjust legislation of the States." The rights to contract, to own property, to inherit, are peculiarly the creatures of State law. It will be recalled that Shellabarger stated, "if the section did in fact assume to define or regulate these civil rights, which are named by the words contract . . . inherit &c., then it would be an assumption of the reserved rights of the States and the people."[92] Thus Shellabarger underscored that the framers had no intention of displacing State control

[89] Id. 117.
[90] Id. 93 (emphasis by Curtis).
[91] Benjamin Kendrick, *The Journal of the Joint Committee on Fifteen on Reconstruction* 46 (1914) (emphasis added).
[92] Supra Chapter 6 text accompanying note 17. See also Curtis supra Chapter 6 note 15.

of those local rights by a national "equal" standard.[93] That only a statewide equality was intended may be gathered from contemporaneous constructions of the cognate due process. In *Walker v. Sauvinet* (1875), the Court declared that due "process in the States is regulated by the law of the State."[94] Justice Bradley went on to say in *Missouri v. Lewis* (1879) that the Fourteenth Amendment "does not profess to secure to all persons in the United States the same laws or the same remedies. Great diversities in these respects may exist in two States separated by an imaginary line. . . . Each State prescribes its own mode of judicial proceeding."[95]

In fine, the 1866 Act, embodied in the Fourteenth Amendment, protected a "limited category" of rights against discrimination. Trumbull's emphasis (reiterated by Wilson and Senator Stewart),[96] that the Act would have no application where the States treated "all alike" with respect thereto, is at war with the creation of "absolute rights." Throughout Curtis ignores the profound impact of (1) the continuing attachment of the North to State control of internal matters, which resulted in a ban on discrimination limited to enumerated rights; and (2) the widespread racism that hobbled improvement of Negro status. A scholarly search of the legislative history must begin with what the framers thought,

[93] During the Ratification campaign, Governor Fletcher of Missouri, as Curtis notes, said that the Fourteenth Amendment "secures to all persons equality of protection . . . under the laws of the State." Curtis, Book 146. See also Shellabarger, supra text accompanying note 83; Trumbull, Chapter 4 at note 11; Stevens, supra text accompanying note 72; and Myers, id. at note 73.

[94] 92 U.S. 90, 93 (1875).

[95] 101 U.S. 22, 31 (1879).

[96] Avins 163–64; supra text accompanying notes 10–12.

not with what Curtis would have them think today.[97] That must be the focus if we would avoid "lawyers' history."[98]

[97] An English scholar, W. R. Brock, wrote, "A belief in racial equality was an abolitionist invention." To "the majority of men in the mid-nineteenth century it seemed to be condemned both by experience and by science." "Even abolitionists were anxious to disclaim any intention of forcing social contacts between the races." W. Brock, *An American Crisis: Congress and Reconstruction* 285, 286 (1963). See also President Lincoln, supra Chapter 5 text accompanying note 60. "Americans clung firmly to a belief in the basic inferiority of the Negro race, a belief supported by the preponderance of nineteenth-century scientific evidence." Paludan, supra note 21 at 54. See also Lincoln, supra note 75.

[98] Maitland wrote that the "process by which old principles and phrases are charged with a new content is from the lawyer's point of view an evolution of the true intent and meaning of the old law; from the historian's point of view it is almost of necessity a process of perversion and misunderstanding." 3 Peter Gay & Victor Wexler, *Historians at Work* 301, 302 (1975).

CHAPTER NINE

John Bingham and Senator Jacob Howard

John Bingham

CURTIS strives mightily to restore the reliability of John Bingham because he is the linchpin of his argument. The "views of Bingham and Howard, leading proponents of the amendment," he asserts, "are entitled to very great weight."[1] But Curtis notes Fairman's conclusion that Bingham was a man of "peculiar conceptions," an "ardent rhetorician, not a man of exact knowledge or accurate language."[2] Fairman was not alone in doubting Bingham. Alexander Bickel charitably wrote that Bingham was "not normally distinguished for precision of thought or statement."[3] Leonard Levy observed that Bingham "was extremely confused and contradictory in his presentation."[4] And Wallace Mendelson concluded that "Bingham is one who used ringing rhetoric as a substitute for analysis."[5] Can it be that Curtis alone perceived the true worth of Bingham, a vision that was

---

[1] Curtis, Book 120. Curtis stresses that "The views of the author of section 1 of the amendment . . . should receive the greatest weight of all." Id. 13.

[2] Id. 121. Curtis cites this for "Bingham was subjected by Fairman to a series of ad hominem attacks." Id. 109.

[3] *Bickel 25.*

[4] L. Levy, *Judgments: Essays on Constitutional History* 77 (1972).

[5] W. Mendelson, "Mr. Justice Black's Fourteenth Amendment," 53 Minn. L. Rev. 711, 716 (1969).

denied to Bickel, Fairman, Levy, Mendelson, and Berger? Let me show Bingham's serious shortcomings.

Bingham's draft of the Fourteenth Amendment provided for "equal protection in the rights of life, liberty, and property," and he stated flatly that "the amendment proposed stands in the very words of the Constitution. . . . *Every word* of the proposed amendment stands in the *very words* of the Constitution."[6] The words "equal protection," however, were *not* in the Constitution; they were added by the Fourteenth Amendment. This is a glaring inexactitude. Bingham was unable to discriminate. Thus he translated the provision of *Article IV (2)* that "the citizens of each State shall be entitled to the privileges and immunities of citizens in the several States" as "*the provision in the bill of rights* that citizens of the United States shall be entitled to all the privileges and immunities of citizens of the United States in the several States."[7] The Bill of Rights contains no privileges and immunities provision. To this Curtis replies that "Bingham never said it did,"[8] but he is squarely contradicted by the quotation. Nor did the framers confuse the rights of a citizen of a State with those of a citizen of the United States; they expressly distinguished between the two.[9]

Bingham, Curtis tells us, "thought the provisions of the Bill of Rights were binding on state officers by their oath and by the privileges and immunities clause of Article IV, section 2."[10] When Article IV was enacted there was no Bill of Rights, so Article IV could not make the unborn Bill of Rights "binding on State officers." And if under *Barron v. Baltimore* the Bill of Rights did not apply to the States, the

---

[6] Avins 150 (emphasis added).
[7] Id. 157 (emphasis added).
[8] Curtis, Book 121.
[9] Supra Chapter 7 text accompanying note 27.
[10] Curtis, Book 64.

oath State officers took to support the Constitution did not bind them to enforce the Bill of Rights against the States. So too, Bingham said, "contrary to the *express* letter of your Constitution 'cruel and unusual punishments' have been inflicted under State laws."[11] The First Amendment's "Congress shall make no law" warns that the Eighth likewise does not apply to the States. Again, Bingham read *Barron* "to show 'that the power of the Federal Government to *enforce* in the United States courts the bill of rights . . . had been denied'."[12] *Barron* held the Bill of Rights inapplicable to the States; it uttered no word about a lack of enforcement power.

Of the same order is Bingham's statement, "If the bill of rights, *as has been solemnly ruled* by the Supreme Court . . . does not limit the power of the States," the

> care of the property, liberty, and the life of the citizen, under the solemn sanction of an oath imposed by your Federal Constitution, is in the States, not in the Federal Government. I have sought to effect no change in that respect. . . . I have advocated here an amendment which would . . . punish all violations by State officers of the Bill of Rights.[13]

If the care of life, liberty, and property "is in the States," how do State officers violate the Bill of Rights, which, Bingham noted, "does not limit the powers of the States." Curtis takes refuge in the word "If," arguing that it shows "Bingham's skepticism about the correctness of *Barron v. Baltimore*."[14] "Solemnly ruled" suggests respect rather than skepticism; and Bingham's "I have sought to effect no change in that respect" has no hypothetical overtones. Bingham was addressing an audience he sought to influence, and his "has

[11] Id. 124 (emphasis added).
[12] Id. 70–71 (emphasis added).
[13] Avins 187 (emphasis added).
[14] Curtis, Book 123.

been solemnly ruled" would lead his fellow lawyers to deduce that the Court had laid down the law, and that could not be shaken by his "skepticism."

Bingham's remarks are rife with contradictions: "I do not admit . . . that any State has a right to disenfranchise any portion of the citizens of the United States";[15] but later he stated, "we all agree . . . that the exercise of the elective franchise, though it be one of the privileges of a citizen of the Republic, is exclusively under the control of the States."[16] If the franchise is indeed a privilege of "a citizen of the Republic," it cannot be "exclusively under the control of the States." Such evidence is dismissed by Curtis as "supposed contradiction."[17] Upon which of Bingham's conflicting utterances did the framers rely? It is a measure of the feebleness of Curtis' cause that he must go to such lengths to rehabilitate Bingham.

One of Curtis' major flaws is his refusal to face up to Bingham's repeated recognition that control of internal matters was left to the States. To escape the impact of one such instance he charged me with "editing" to produce "a decidedly misleading effect," illustrating the "dangers of selective quotation."[18] In a footnote buried at the back of his book, he explains that my "omission occurred based on a mistaken assumption";[19] consequently, his pejorative "decidedly misleading" and "selective quotation," which connote intentional suppression, disclose him to be a propagandist

[15] Globe App. 57.

[16] Globe 2542. So Trumbull stated, supra chapter 6 note 17; see also Howard, supra Chapter 8 note 77.

[17] Curtis, Book 121. Bingham considered that enfranchisement of the blacks conformed "exactly to the spirit of the Constitution and according to the declared intent of the Framers." Globe 430. In fact, the Constitution protected slavery. Supra Chapter 5 text accompanying notes 87–88.

[18] Curtis, Book 122–23.

[19] Id. 249. This extenuation would with better grace have been inserted in the text to defuse the noisome accusation.

rather than a dispassionate historian. With apologies to the weary reader, I must examine such trivia because they exemplify the tactics that have taken in respected scholars, let alone that they tarnish my reputation. My "edited" version follows:

> The care of the property, the liberty, and the life of the citizen . . . is *in the States,* and not in the Federal Government. I have sought to effect no change in that respect . . . I have advocated here an amendment which would arm Congress with the power to punish all violations of the bill of rights. . . . I have always believed that *protection* . . . within the States of all the rights of person and citizen, was of the power *reserved to the States.*[20]

What Bingham "actually said" was:

> The care of the property, the liberty, and the life of the citizen, *under the solemn sanction of an oath imposed by your Federal Constitution,* is in the States and not in the Federal Government. I have sought to effect no change in that respect in the Constitution of the country. I have advocated here an amendment which would arm Congress with the power *to compel obedience to the oath,* and punish all violations by State officers of the Bill of Rights, *but leaving those officers to discharge the duties enjoined upon them as citizens of the United States and by the Constitution.*[21] (emphasis in the original)

My "misleading omission" was to "leave out Bingham's qualification, which was, essentially, that the care of the life, property, and liberty of the citizen, *subject to constitutional limitations* [i.e., the oath] is in the States."[22] The "limitations" are a figment of Curtis' imagination. In the very same speech, Bingham, without qualification, said, "I have always believed that the protection . . . within the States of all the rights of person and property was of the powers reserved to

[20] Curtis, Book 122–23.
[21] Id. 123.
[22] Id. (emphasis added).

the States. And so I still believe."[23] He proceeded on the false assumption that the Bill of Rights applied to the States in the teeth of *Barron v. Baltimore,* the assumption, as Curtis puts it, "that [his] constitutional views and those of a number of his colleagues, not the decisions of the Supreme Court, accurately stated the law."[24] It may not be assumed that the sober lawyers who listened to him preferred his version of the law to that of the Supreme Court. Like Lincoln, who knew that the Court's decisions did not vanish because deemed objectionable, but must be overruled by the Court or by amendment, as the Framers did explicitly with respect to *Dred Scott,*[25] they cannot be saddled with Bingham's view. His disavowal of any intention to "take away from any State any right that belongs to it" was calculated to allay fears of undue interference with States Rights. Nor does this excerpt stand alone. To Robert Hale's statement that "the citizen must rely upon the States for their protection," Bingham replied, "I admit that such is the rule under the Constitution as it now stands," and underscored the point by reading to the House Madison's assurance in the Federalist that internal matters were reserved to the States, emphasizing "that this is the text of the Constitution."[26] So my "misleading omission" of Bingham's "subject to constitutional limitations" turns out by his own testimony to be no "*constitutional* limitation" at all.

Bingham further illustrates the folly of inflating the influ-

---

[23] Avins 188.

[24] Curtis, Book 63.

[25] Id. 215.

[26] Avins 159. Curtis quotes Bingham's rejection of an intention "to take away from any State any rights that belongs to it. . . . The proposition pending before the House is simply a proposition to arm the Congress . . . with the power to enforce the bill of rights *as it stands in the Constitution today.* It 'hath that extent—no more'." Curtis, Book 95 (emphasis added) (another example of Bingham's befuddlement).

ence of the "antislavery origins of the amendment," which
Curtis asserts, it was Fairman's "major fault" to overlook.[27]
In 1859, for example, Bingham had opposed the admission
of Oregon because its Constitution forbade the entry of a
"free negro or mulatto" into the State.[28] But in 1866 he led
the fight against Radical opposition to the readmission of
Tennessee because its constitution did not provide for Negro
enfranchisement, and prevailed by a vote of 125 to 12.[29] He
had been defeated in 1862 and reelected in 1864;[30] David
Donald states that he "was fully aware that his Ohio District
could easily go Democratic, since his own average from 1862
to 1870 was only 50.6 percent of the total. Bitterly he protested against Radical proposals for 'universal suffrage'."[31]
His political instincts did not betray him, for in the April
1867 elections "Ohio overwhelmed a negro suffrage amendment by 40,000."[32] This was the State in which Senator
John Sherman said, "We do not like Negroes. We do not
conceal our dislike."[33] Not only had Northern goals shifted
after the abolition of slavery, but political realities had di-
luted Bingham's early zeal. To prate against this background

[27] Curtis, Book 100, 42. Leonard Levy anticipated Curtis in concluding
that "the evidence of 1866–1868 must be read in the light of a received
tradition of abolitionist constitutional argument." Levy, supra note 4 at
70. Fairman erred, Levy opined, in construing "the words used . . . in a
lawyer's terms. He therefore missed the history that was behind those
words," words that "can be appreciated only by understanding them and
the language of the amendment as expressions of the constitutional ideology of the abolitionists." Levy, id. 69–70. For detailed refutation of
this view, see supra Chapter 5 text accompanying notes 72–102.

[28] Curtis, Book 59.

[29] Globe 3979, 3980.

[30] Curtis, Book 248 note 212.

[31] D. Donald, *The Politics of Reconstruction* 46 (1965).

[32] C. V. Woodward, "Seeds of Failure in Radical Race Policy," in *New
Frontiers of American Reconstruction* 137 (H. Hyman ed. 1966).

[33] Id. 128.

of the impact of abolitionist theology on the Amendment is to prefer fantasy to fact.

SENATOR JACOB HOWARD

Senator Jacob Howard is, with Bingham, one of the pillars of Curtis' case, as he was of Justice Black's. Due to the sudden illness of Chairman Fessenden, it fell to Howard to act as spokesman for the Joint Committee, saying, "I can only promise to present to the Senate . . . the views and motives which influenced that committee, so far as I understand those views and motives."[34] This does not pretend to be the Committee's official view but merely Howard's impression thereof. Curtis to the contrary notwithstanding, Howard did *not* have "charge of the amendment in the Senate."[35] Up to this point his participation in the debates on the Civil Rights Bill and the several aspects of the Amendment had been negligible. Nor were his views fine-tuned to those of Bingham. Fairman recounts that "Howard apparently had not entered into the spirit of Bingham's drafting: three times in the committee he had voted against the author's work."[36] According to Benjamin Kendrick, author of the Journal of the Joint Reconstruction Committee, Howard was "one of the most . . . reckless of the radicals," who had served consistently "in the vanguard of the extreme Negrophiles,"[37] in which he was certainly far removed from the pervasive racism of the North. He and Elisha Washburne "had been the only Republicans to hold out for black suf-

[34] Avins 218–19.

[35] Curtis, Book 115 (emphasis added).

[36] 6 Charles Fairman, *History of the Supreme Court of the United States* 1291 (1971).

[37] B. Kendrick, *The Journal of the Joint Committee of Fifteen on Reconstruction* 257, 192 (1914).

frage to the end, all the others proved willing to abandon it."[38] Howard's "attitude tended to be more radical and purely partisan than that of Fessenden."[39] That such a man could speak "for" a "non-radical Joint Committee,"[40] in which by Fessenden's testimony there "was very considerable difference of opinion,"[41] strains credulity. How little Howard's loose utterances are to be trusted is underlined by his statement that the Amendment "abolishes *all* class legislation in the States" in the teeth of the framers' repeated rejection of attempts to prohibit *all* manner of discrimination.[42]

In the midst of a very long speech, Howard read an extract from *Corfield v. Coryell* and said, "to those privileges and immunities should be added the personal rights guaranteed and secured by the first eight amendments."[43] Like Bingham, who recognized that *Barron v. Baltimore* "solemnly ruled" that the Bill of Rights "did not limit the power of the States," (yet considered that it was enforceable) "by the oath State officers took to support the Constitution,"[44] Howard perceived that the Bill of Rights does "not operate in the slightest degree as a restraint or prohibition upon the State legislatures. States are not affected by them." Nevertheless, the Bill was to be enforced "by the fifth section of this amendment which declares that 'the Congress shall have power to enforce by appropriate legislation the *provisions* of this article'."[45] Historically, we have seen, "privileges or immunities" drawn from Article IV (2) did not embrace the

[38] M. L. Benedict, *A Compromise of Principle* 170 (1975); James 82.
[39] James 135.
[40] Benedict, supra note 38 at 37, 34.
[41] Avins 211.
[42] Id. 220; Berger, *Judiciary* 163–64.
[43] Avins 219.
[44] Supra Chapter 8 text accompanying note 13, and Chapter 6 text accompanying note 98.
[45] Avins 219, 220, (emphasis added).

then unborn Bill of Rights. A contemporary decision of the Supreme Court declared that "The amendment did not add to the privileges and immunities of a citizen."[46] Section 5 did not purport to enlarge the "provisions" of the amendment but only to furnish the means of enforcing them. Are we to conclude that the able lawyers who listened to Howard concurred in Howard's patently fallacious conclusion that Congress was authorized to "enforce" upon the States a provision that did not bind them?

Curtis notes that "There was no extended discussion of section one," but urges that "after Howard spoke" "*Not a single senator or congressman contradicted him.*"[47] The Senators who had been categorically assured by Lyman Trumbull, chairman of the Senate Judiciary Committee, of the limited scope of privileges and immunities, and who probably were aware of similar expressions in the House shortly before Howard spoke,[48] presumably felt no need to contradict one of many Howard assertions. "Republican members of the Senate," Joseph James found, "refrained from defining their positions on the floor. . . . Their actions in the Senate were mostly confined to voting."[49] Even so, shortly after Howard spoke, Senator Luke Poland said that the clause "secures *nothing beyond* what was intended by the original [Article IV] provision in the Constitution,"[50] which antedated and therefore could not comprehend the Bill of Rights. Doubtless *some* Republicans, Bingham among others, "went beyond the conventional reading of Article IV,"

[46] Supra Chapter 7 text accompanying note 38; see also Bingham, id. text accompanying note 45.

[47] Curtis, Book 89, 91, (emphasis in original). Levy dismisses the assumption that "silence on the part of their opponents signified acquiescence." Levy, supra note 4 at 68.

[48] Infra note 52.

[49] James, supra note 38 at 146.

[50] Avins 230.

but it does not follow that "Poland's remarks did not reflect the intent of the framers."[51] Poland, I daresay, was closer to their thinking[52] than the arch-radical Howard.

A few days after Howard spoke, Senator Timothy Howe, a "Radical,"[53] urging adoption of the privileges or immunities clause of the Amendment, and echoing his earlier statement, referred to the South's determination, balked by the military occupation, to deny to blacks

> the plainest and most necessary rights of citizenship. The right to hold land when they bought and paid for it would have been denied them; the right to collect their wages by the processes of law when they earned their wages; the right to appear in court as suitors for any wrong done them or any right denied them, the right to give testimony in any court . . . all these rights would have been denied.[54]

Those rights, specifically written into the Civil Rights Bill in response to the Black Codes, patently remained the framers' concern when they turned to the Amendment, which

---

[51] Curtis, Book 127.

[52] Poland echoed narrowing explanations in the House only two weeks before Howard spoke. James Garfield stated that the amendment proposed to put the Civil Rights Bill "beyond the reach of the plots and machinations of any party." Avins 213. Thayer said, "it is but incorporating in the Constitution . . . the principles of the civil rights bill which has lately become a law," in order that it "shall be forever incorporated into the Constitution of the United States." Id. John Broomall remarked, "it may be asked, why should we put a provision in the Constitution which is already contained in an act of Congress"; he "wished to prevent a mere majority from repealing the law." Id. 214. Henry Raymond observed that by the Bill "Congress proposed to exercise precisely the powers which that amendment was intended to confer." Id. 214. Howard himself stated that the amendment was designed to "give validity" to the Civil Rights Act. Id. 228.

[53] Supra Chapter 2 note 25.

[54] Avins 231.

they considered to be "identical" with the Bill,[55] as Howe's audience was well aware. Where is the evidence that the framers intended to enlarge the goals of the Bill? Howe's remarks bespeak identity, not change. The fact is that the prevailing racism and attachment to States' Rights speak against such an unexplained change.

Senator Poland observed that "Great differences have existed among ourselves; many opinions have had to yield to enable us to agree upon a plan."[56] He is corroborated by Senator Fessenden, the chairman of the Joint Committee:

> Unquestionably in the committee there was very considerable difference of opinion. That difference of opinion had to be reconciled. . . . [T]he committee, after much deliberation, came to the conclusion that its duty was to agree upon that which seemed the best scheme with regard to reconstruction upon which they would come to a unanimous or nearly unanimous agreement.[57]

Now, after the compromise of such differences and the expression of the reconciliation in explicit terms, Curtis would have us believe on the basis of Howard's remark that the framers threw the carefully wrought compromises into the discard and blindly accepted Howard's position, that of a "most reckless Radical," entailing a sweeping encroachment on the domain of Northern States.

Were Howard's remarks, contrary to the fact, representative of majority opinion in the Senate, it would remain to inquire whether they reflected opinion in the House. After

[55] Supra note 52. Senator Cowen, who spoke not long before Howard, said "That all people should have the right to contract, I agree. That all people should have the right to enforce their contracts, I agree. . . . I would allow them to purchase, hold, and lease, and to be entitled to their remedies for the defense of their property." Avins 202.

[56] Globe 2964.

[57] Avins 211.

Howard spoke, George Latham said that "the 'civil rights bill' which is now a law . . . *covers exactly the same ground* as this amendment."[58] Thereafter William Windom, a "Radical," summarized the Amendment as meaning "Your life shall be spared, your liberty shall be unabridged, your property shall be protected."[59] Viewed most generously, Howard's remarks are met by countervailing views, so that they do not constitute satisfactory evidence of the framers' intent. More important, Leonard Levy, "whose encouragement," Curtis tells us, "has been constant and crucial,"[60] wrote, "there is no reason to believe that Bingham and Howard expressed the view of the majority of Congress."[61]

[58] Id. 223.

[59] Curtis' citation to Windom's reference to a purpose to secure "all the rights of citizenship," Curtis, Book 89–90, should be juxtaposed with this statement. Compare Windom's remarks, supra Chapter 8 text accompanying note 11.

[60] Curtis, Book xi.

[61] Levy, supra note 4 at 77. When Howard's remarks were cited to the Court in Maxwell v. Dow, 176 U.S. 581, 601 (1899), it said, "It is clear that what is said in Congress upon such an occasion may or may not express the majority of those who favor the adoption of the measure," and it demanded evidence of "what construction was given to it, if any, by other members of Congress."

Alfred Kelly, himself an activist apologist, explained that the Radicals were reluctant to take the majority into their confidence. He noted a "curious ambiguity . . . in the Radical's advocacy of the measure. . . . It was as though the Radical leaders were avoiding a precise delineation of legal consequences," this on the basis of their resort to the "technique of lofty, expansive and highly generalized language." Why?

> there was a substantial block of moderate Republicans who had not yet committed themselves entirely to the Radical position. . . . If [the Radicals] drove home too far the proposition that this amendment would undoubtedly consummate the destruction of all caste and class legislation . . . moderate Republican support might be alienated and the requisite two-thirds majority necessary to the amendment's adoption might not be obtained. Political strategy called for ambiguity not clarity.

In truth, the evidence compels the contrary conclusion—that the majority rejected their views.[62]

The foregoing by no means exhaust the list of Curtis' shortcomings; to do so would merely pile up cumulative evidence and needlessly tax the patience of the reader. Instead, let me turn to Curtis' belittling remarks about the scholarship of Charles Fairman, whose "incorporation" study, wrote William Nelson, is "a now classic,"[63] "whose research," wrote Harold Hyman, "shaped much of the constitutional field,"[64] and who was chosen to treat the Reconstruction period of the *History of the Supreme Court* under the bequest of Justice Holmes.[65] To argue that Fairman *"overlooked much evidence that tended to contradict his thesis"*[66] is to suggest purposeful suppression. Again, Fairman, Curtis charges, "found clarity from the Democrats. Michael C. Kerr, Indiana Democrat . . . noted that the [fifth] amendment has limited only the federal government, not the states,

---

A. Kelly, "The Fourteenth Amendment Reconsidered: The Segregation Question," 54 Mich. L. Rev. 1049, 1084 (1956).

Bingham had protested against the "oppressive" scope of the Civil Rights Bill, and Curtis has yet to explain why Bingham embraced precisely that "oppressive" effect in the Amendment. Could Bingham have conspired to hoodwink the Ratifiers and shield himself from retribution? If so, lacking full disclosure of material facts, the ratification would be invalid. Berger, *Judiciary* 155 note 93. Although I consider that the majority knowingly employed words of art of established and limited meaning, Kelly underlines my view that the Radical views were not those of the majority. Nor can the rights reserved to the States be defeated by "ambiguous" terms. That calls for expression of a clear intention to do so.

[62] Supra chapter 5 text accompanying notes 94–101.

[63] William Nelson, "History and Neutrality in Constitution Adjudication," 72 Va. L. Rev. 1237, 1253 (1986). Curtis refers to Fairman's "massive study of the Supreme Court during reconstruction." Curtis, Book 93.

[64] H. Hyman, "Federalism: Legal Fiction and Historical Artifact?" 1987 Brigham Young Law Review 905, 924.

[65] Supra note 63.

[66] Curtis, Book 6.

and cited Barron v. Baltimore."[67] To Curtis this indicates that "something is askew,"[68] an ill-disguised attempt to tar Fairman as a Democratic sympathizer, as if an incontrovertible fact becomes less so when stated by a Democrat. Consider also, "To Fairman's *dismay*, Trumbull quoted Corfield and Story as to privileges or immunities as though the two were inconsistent"; "Fairman was *horrified* at the thought that the fourteenth amendment might require the states to obey all of the Bill of Rights."[69] Meticulous scholar that he is, Fairman would not be "dismayed" or "horrified" because the facts did not tidily fit a preconceived theory, but would bow to the facts, as is the prime duty of a scholar.

After 55 years of dedication to scholarship, I may be permitted to notice Curtis' charges that "Berger's work is riddled with errors of fact and interpretation," "grossly inaccurate," contains "obvious misstatements"; his "historical analysis" is "so mistaken that it is entitled to little weight."[70] Let Alexander Bickel speak for me. Of an earlier book he wrote that Berger's "analysis is independent and rigorous and so his book offers much fresh interpretation and insight. . . . He is always deeply informed and powerful and altogether convincing . . . a distinguished work."[71] To those who may consider that I am unduly harsh on Curtis, I may say, like Edward Gibbon, "I have tediously acquired by a painful perusal, the right of pronouncing this unfavorable sentence."[72]

[67] Id. 97; see also id. 94, 100.

[68] Id. 100.

[69] Id. 93, 5.

[70] M. Curtis, "Judge Hand's History: An Analysis of History and Method in *Jaffree v. Board of School Commissioners of Mobile County.*" 86 W. Va. L. Rev. 109, 124 (1983); Curtis, *Reply* 47.

[71] A. Bickel, "Book Review" 73 Am. Hist. Rev. 1509, 1510 (1970).

[72] E. Gibbon, *The History of the Decline and Fall of the Roman Empire* 60 note 11 (Nottingham ed. undated).

Conclusion

THE Fourteenth Amendment constituted an attempt to rescue the emancipated blacks from a return to bondage, hammered out in a racist atmosphere by Northern States jealous of incursions into *their* sovereignty. It did not purport, as Senator Fessenden and Thaddeus Stevens lamented, to abolish *all* discriminations. At the outset Stevens had sought to ban all discrimination, saying that proposition "is the one I love: that is the one which I hope, before we separate, we shall have educated ourselves up to the idea of adopting, and that we shall have educated our people up to the point of ratifying."[1] Stevens' recognition of the need to *educate* Congress and the people to ban *all* discriminations testifies that abolitionist theology had made small impact. In the end, Stevens settled for less, notwithstanding he had hoped that the people

> would have so remodelled all our institutions as to have freed them from every vestige of . . . inequality of rights . . . that no distinction would be tolerated. . . . This bright dream has vanished. . . . We shall be obliged to be content with patching up the worst portions of the ancient edifice.[2]

The cochairman of the Joint Committee, Senator Fessenden, also recognized that "We cannot put into the Constitu-

---

[1] Avins 133.
[2] Id. 237.

tion, owing to existing prejudices and existing institutions [i.e., racism and States rights] an entire exclusion of all distinctions."[3] No reference to these remarks will be found in Curtis' opus. He turned his back on the most potent influences that served to limit the scope of the Amendment.[4]

A long-standing guide to construction is: what was the mischief the draftsmen sought to remedy.[5] The Civil Rights Bill, which both the framers and Ratifiers stated was "identical" with the Amendment, was fueled by the Black Codes' attempt to return the emancipated slaves to serfdom, accompanied by a campaign of flogging, murder, and terrorism. When the framers and Ratifiers spoke of equal protection it was against such violence that they meant to protect the helpless blacks.[6] To enable the freedmen to exist, they granted them the right to contract for their labor, to own property, to go freely from place to place—denied them by the Codes—and to sue for enforcement of these rights.

The words employed in the Amendment were not glittering generalities; but for "equal protection" they had historic content; they were what lawyers term "words of art," tech-

[3] Globe 705.

[4] Curtis' own "authority," Harold Hyman, wrote that "Negrophobia" held Reconstruction "at low throttle," and that "a heavy phalanx of Republican politicos, including Sherman and Trumbull . . . were states rights nationalists, suspicious of any new functional path the nation travelled." H. Hyman, *A More Perfect Union* 447, 304 (1973).

[5] "Under principles coming down from Heydon's Case [3 Co. Rep. 7a, 76 Eng. Rep. 637 (1584)] a court faced with the task of construction must endeavor to appreciate the mischief the framers were seeking to alleviate." Henry Friendly, "The Bill of Rights as a Code of Criminal Procedure," 53 Calif. L. Rev. 929, 943 (1965). For additinal citations, see Raoul Berger, *Congress v. The Supreme Court* 220 note 95 (1969).

[6] Alexander Bickel concluded that "the Senate moderates, led by Trumbull and Fessenden," viewed "a right to equal protection in the literal sense of benefitting equally from the laws for the security of person and property." Bickel 56.

nical terms. For centuries "due process of law" had meant that a defendant was entitled to judicial process that was "due," i.e., customary. "Privileges or immunities" had their origin in the Articles of Confederation, and were picked up by Article IV (2) of the Constitution. A number of courts had construed them narrowly, as Senator Trumbull remarked to the framers. In lieu of "privileges and immunities" the Civil Rights Bill had employed "civil rights and immunities," followed by a few particularized privileges. This phrase incensed Bingham, the putative draftsman of the Amendment, who vehemently disapproved of the "oppressive" invasion of the States' domain. In deference to his protest, the words "civil rights and immunities" were deleted, in order, Wilson explained, to avoid a "latitudinarian construction not intended." After reviewing this history the Supreme Court concluded, "the legislative history of the 1866 Act clearly indicates that Congress intended to protect a limited category of rights."[7]

The argument that these "limited" rights were tersely encapsulated in the Amendment rests not only on the repeated, never contradicted, assertion that Act and Amendment were identical, but also on the thus far unanswered question: why did Bingham come to embrace in the Amendment what he had roundly condemned as "oppressive" in the Civil Rights Bill? The limited scope of the Amendment was repeatedly emphasized during the Ratification campaign. Then too, there is the undeniable racism that threatened officials who went too far in behalf of blacks, limiting the framers to outlawing terrorism in the South, with never an intimation in the course of the Ratification campaign that the North also must accept federal intrusion into local administration. Where is the clearly expressed intention—on

[7] Georgia v. Rachel, 384 U.S. 780, 791 (1966).

which Chief Justice Marshall insisted—to curtail Northern control of its own destiny, and under cover of "equal protection" and "privileges or immunities" to extend federal intervention in local affairs to an undreamed-of extent?[8] Against the historical evidence, "equal protection" has become a crystal ball in which judicial soothsayers can find whatever they will.[9]

[8] Protesting against regarding a corporation as a "person" for purposes of the Fourteenth Amendment, Justice Black stated (I substitute "criminal administration" for his "corporation"):

> The States did not adopt the Amendment with knowledge of its sweeping meaning under its present construction. No section of the Amendment gave notice to the people that, if adopted, it would subject every state law . . . affecting [criminal administration] . . . to censorship of the United States courts. No word in all this Amendment gave any hint that its adoption would deprive the states of their long recognized power to regulate [criminal administration].

Connecticut General Insurance Co. v. Johnson, 303 U.S. 77, 89 (1935), dissenting opinion. Referring to grand jury indictments, trial by jury of twelve, etc., Justice Frankfurter said:

> It would be extraordinarily strange for a Constitution to convey such specific commands in such a roundabout and inexplicit way. . . . Those reading the English language with the meaning it ordinarily conveys . . . would hardly recognize the Fourteenth Amendment as a cover for the various explicit provisions of the first eight amendments.

Adamson v. California, 322 U.S. 46, 63 (1947), concurring opinion. Horace Flack concluded, "had the people been informed of what was intended by the amendment, they would have rejected it." Flack 237. See Alfred Kelly, supra Chapter 9 note 61.

[9] Philip Kurland stated, "The new equal protection . . . is the old substantive due process. . . . The difference between the new equal protection and old substantive due process is essentially the difference in the hierarchy of values of the Court." "Forum: Equal Protection and the Burger Court," 2 Hastings Const. L.Q. 645, 661 (1975). Herbert Packer pointed out that "the new 'substantive equal protection' has under a different label permitted today's Justices to impose their prejudices in much the same manner as the Four Horsemen once did." H. Packer, "The Aim

At stake is the integrity of the Constitution, the right of the people to govern themselves, for instance, to require death penalties even though they offend the sensibilities of the Justices.[10] Whence does the Court derive authority to bring the Constitution in tune with its own predilections? Its sense of justice may for the moment reflect our own, but as Justice Cardozo observed, to substitute it for the will of the framers "might result in a benevolent despotism if the judges were benevolent men. It would put an end to the rule of law."[11] Just now these views are unfashionable in aca-

of the Criminal Law Revisited: A Plea for a Look at 'Substantive Due Process'," 44 S. Cal. L. Rev. 490, 491–92 (1971).

For a detailed discussion of the roots of "equal protection" in the framers' aim to outlaw discrimination with respect to the rights granted by the Civil Rights Bill, see Berger, *Judiciary* 170, 166–92.

[10] Consider Justice Brennan's acknowledgment that his view that death penalties constitute a "cruel and unusual punishment" is "an interpretation to which a majority of my fellow Justices [seven]—not to mention, it would seem, a majority of my fellow countrymen [about 70%] does not subscribe." Yet he steadfastly maintains his view in dissent after dissent, hoping "to embody a community striving for human dignity for all, although perhaps not yet arrived." "Address," October 12, 1985, reprinted in *The Great Debate: Interpreting Our Written Constitution* II, 24 (Washington, Federalist Society, 1986). Were Brennan in the majority, he would be cramming his "view" down the throat of a dissenting public—illustrating what government by judiciary means.

In a 1987 speech at Harvard Law School, Judge Richard Posner said that

> a judge ought not to substitute personal values for those that are part of the "text, structure and history" of the Constitution. As an example, he argued that judges should not interpret the Constitution to bar the death penalty. Capital punishment was common when the Eighth Amendment was adopted, is supported by 75 percent of the nation, and can be supported by evidence of its deterrent effect.

38 Harv. L. Bull. 34 (1987).

[11] B. N. Cardozo, *The Nature of the Judicial Process* 136 (1921). Justice Harlan declared, "When the Court disregards the express intent and

deme. But when I deflated the alleged impact of antislavery theology on the Fourteenth Amendment, which had been heralded by Jacobus tenBroek and Howard Jay Graham, and is now applauded by Curtis and Leonard Levy,[12] Lord Beloff, an Oxford emeritus and longtime student of American constitutionalism, concurred, saying, "The quite extraordinary contortions that have gone into proving the contrary make sad reading for those impressed by the high quality of American legal-historical scholarship."[13] The present attempt by academicians to find in the Amendment what they want to believe stands no higher, and it will not, I predict, be viewed in the future as their shining hour.

All this may seem like tilting at windmills at a time when Judge Robert Bork, during the hearings on his nomination to the Supreme Court, felt constrained to say that too many expectations had crystallized around the incorporation doctrine to permit its disturbance. That, to my mind, is particularly inappropriate at this juncture when we purport to celebrate the bicentennial of the written Constitution rather than the judicial barnacles with which it has become encrusted.[14] The struggle for a written Constitution, Justice Black justly stated, was "to make certain that men in power

---

understanding of the Framers, it has invaded the realm of the political process to which the amending power was committed, and it has violated the constitutional structure which is its highest duty to protect." Oregon v. Mitchell, 400 U.S. 112, 202–03 (1970).

[12] Curtis, Book III; L. Levy, *Judgments: Essays in American Constitutional History* 70 (1972).

[13] Max Beloff, "Book Review," The Times (London) April 7, 1978 (Higher Education Supplement at 11).

[14] Compare Solicitor General Robert Jackson's paean to the then reemergence of the constitutional text from beneath a laissez faire gloss, analogizing it to the rediscovery of an Old Master after the retouching brushwork of succeeding generations had been removed. R. Jackson, "Back to the Constitution," 25 A.B.A.J. 745, 748 (1939).

would be governed by law, not by the arbitrary fiat of the man or men in power."[15]

It is difficult for me to regard the precedents of the last 40 years as more sacrosanct than those of the prior 135 years during which, as Louis Henkin reminded us, the exemption of the States from the Bill of Rights had been "the consistent, often reaffirmed, and almost unanimous jurisprudence of the Court."[16] Adverse possession does not run against the government, still less against the sovereign people; usurpation is not legitimated by inertia.[17] The contrary view, as Willard Hurst said in an analogous context, would simply be "a way of practically reading Article V out of the Constitution."[18] The fact is, as Leonard Levy noted, that "at no time in our history have the American people passed judgment, pro or con, on the merits of judicial review over Congress."[19] How could they ratify judicial revision of the Constitution when they were repeatedly told that, as Frankfurter wrote to Franklin Roosevelt, "when the Supreme Court speaks it is not they who speak but the Constitution."[20]

Were the Court endowed with the power of divining the

[15] *In re* Winship, 397 U.S. 358, 384 (1970), dissenting opinion.

[16] Supra chapter 1 text accompanying note 12.

[17] "Non-existent power" can not be "prescripted by an unchallenged exercise." United States v. Morton Salt Co., 338 U.S. 632, 647 (1950). Sir Frederick Pollock wrote to Justice Holmes, "Strange that a proved series of blunders should be more sacred than one." 1 *Holmes-Pollock Letters* 239 (1946).

[18] W. Hurst, "Discussion," in *Supreme Court and Supreme Law* 74 (E. Cahn ed. 1954). Learned Hand also adhered to amendment as the proper means of change. Kathryn Griffith, *Judge Learned Hand and the Role of the Federal Judiciary* 83 (1975). Justice Hugo Black rang the changes on this theme, e.g., in Griswold v. Connecticut, 381 U.S. 479, 522 (1965).

[19] L. Levy, *Judicial Review and the Supreme Court* 3 (1967).

[20] *Roosevelt and Frankfurter: Their Correspondence, 1928–1945* 381 (M. Freedman ed. 1967).

public desire—contrary to its course in the death penalty cases—it would yet run afoul of Hamilton's assurance to the Ratifiers:

> Until the people have, by some solemn and authoritative act, annulled or changed the established law, it is binding upon themselves collectively as well as individually; and no presumption, or even knowledge of their sentiments, can warrant their representatives in a departure from it, prior to such an act.[21]

Finally, *Erie Ry. Co. v. Tompkins* reversed the 100-year-old course of *Swift v. Tyson*, about which many "expectations" of the commercial and financial communities had gathered in the course of a century, because, in the words of Justice Brandeis, quoting Justice Holmes, it was "an unconstitutional assumption of power by courts of the United States which no lapse of time or respectable array of opinion should make us hesitate to correct."[22] Celebration of the Bicentennial of the Constitution calls on us to exhibit no less hardihood and to respect its integrity, i.e., its "original meaning."

[21] Federalist No. 78 at 509 (Mod. Lib. ed. 1937). In the First Congress, Madison said "sovereignty of the people" means "the people can change the Constitution if they please; but while the Constitution exists, they must conform themselves to its dictates." 1 *Ann. Cong.* 739 (1st Cong., 1st Sess., Gales & Seaton 1834) (print bearing running head "History of Congress").

[22] Erie Ry. Co. v. Tompkins, 304 U.S. 64, 79 (1938).

Doubtless I shall be charged with inconsistency because I wrote that it would be "probably impossible to undo the past in the face of the expectations that the segregation decisions . . . have aroused in our black citizens—expectations confirmed by every decent instinct." Berger, *Judiciary* 412–13; Raoul Berger, *Death Penalties: The Supreme Court's Obstacle Course* 179–80 (1982). But the rank discrimination against blacks cannot be equated with equal application of the procedural safeguards of the Bill of Rights which, if they be applicable to the States, protect whites and blacks alike. To leave electronic wire-tapping to the States, for instance, is not of the same order as a return to Jim Crowism. The latter would be met by widespread resistance, an altogether unlikely consequence were wire-tapping returned to the States.

Bibliography

BOOKS

Adams, Henry. *John Randolph* (Boston, Houghton Mifflin, 1882).

Adams, J. Donald. *Copey at Harvard* (Boston, Houghton Mifflin, 1960).

Avins, Alfred. *The Reconstruction Amendments' Debates* (Richmond, Va., Virginia Commission on Constitutional Government, 1967).

Benedict, Michael L. *A Compromise of Principle* (New York, Norton, 1975).

Berger, Raoul, *Congress v. The Supreme Court* (Cambridge, Mass., Harvard University Press, 1969).

———. *Government by Judiciary: The Transformation of the Fourteenth Amendment* (Cambridge, Mass., Harvard University Press, 1977).

———. *Death Penalties: The Supreme Court's Obstacle Course* (Cambridge, Mass., Harvard University Press, 1982).

———. *Federalism: The Founders' Design* (Norman, University of Oklahoma Press, 1987).

Bickel, Alexander. *The Least Dangerous Branch* (Indianapolis, Bobbs Merrill, 1962).

———. *The Supreme Court and the Idea of Progress* (New York, Harper & Row, 1970).

Blackstone, William. *Commentaries on the Laws of England* (London, 1765–1769).

Brock, William. *An American Crisis: Congress and Reconstruction* (London, Macmillan, 1963).

Brodie, Fawn. *Thaddeus Stevens: The Scourge of the South* (New York, Norton, 1959).

Cardozo, Benjamin N. *The Nature of the Judicial Process* (New Haven, Yale University Press, 1921).

Commager, Henry S. *Documents of American History* (7th ed., New York, Appleton, 1963).

Corwin, Edward S. *The Twilight of the Supreme Court* (New Haven, Yale University Press, 1934).

Crosskey, William. *Politics and the Constitution in the History of the United States* (Chicago, University of Chicago Press, 1953).

Donald, David. *The Politics of Reconstruction* (Baton Rouge, Louisiana State University Press, 1965).

———. *Charles Sumner and the Rights of Man* (New York, Knopf, 1970).

Ely, John H. *Democracy and Distrust* (Cambridge, Mass., Harvard University Press, 1980).

Farrand, Max. *The Records of the Federal Convention 1787* (New Haven, Yale University Press, 1911).

The Federalist (New York, Modern Library ed. 1937).

Fehrenbacher, Don E. *The Dred Scott Case: Its Significance in American Law and Policy* (New York, Oxford University Press, 1978).

Fairman, Charles. *History of the Supreme Court of the United States,* vol. 6 (New York, Macmillan, 1971).

Flack, Horace. *The Adoption of the Fourteenth Amendment* (Baltimore, Johns Hopkins University Press, 1908).

Frankfurter, Felix. *The Commerce Clause* (Chapel Hill, University of North Carolina Press, 1937).

———. *Law and Policy* (New York, Harcourt Brace, 1938).

———. *Felix Frankfurter Reminisces,* H. R. Phillips ed. (New York, Reynal, 1960).

Gay, Peter and Wexler, Victor. *Historians at Work* (New York, Harper & Row, 1975).

Gibbon, Edward. *Decline and Fall of the Roman Empire* (Nottingham ed. undated).

Gillette, William. *The Right to Vote: Politics and the Passage of the Fifteenth Amendment* (Baltimore, Johns Hopkins University Press, 1965).

Graham, Howard J. *Everyman's Constitution* (New York, Norton, 1968).

Griffin, Kathryn. *Judge Learned Hand and the Role of the Federal Judiciary* (Norman, University of Oklahoma Press, (1975).

Haines, Charles. *The American Doctrine of Judicial Supremacy* (New York, Russell & Russell, 1959).

Hamilton, Alexander. *The Papers of Alexander Hamilton*. H. Syrett and J. Cooke, eds. (New York, Columbia University Press, 1962).

Hamilton, Walton, and Adair, Douglas. *The Power to Govern* (New York, Norton, 1973).

Hand, Learned. *The Spirit of Liberty*. I. Dillard, ed. (New York, Knopf, 1952).

Hirst, F. A.. *Early Life and Letters of John Morley* (London, Macmillan, 1927).

Hook, Sidney. *Philosophy and Public Policy* (Carbondale, Southern Illinois University Press, 1980).

Hyman, H. M. *A More Perfect Union* (New York, Knopf, 1973).

Hyndman, H. M. *Further Reminiscences* (London, Macmillan, 1912).

James, Joseph. *The Framing of the Fourteenth Amendment* (Urbana, University of Illinois Press, 1965).

Keller, Morton. *Affairs of State* (Cambridge, Mass., Harvard University Press, 1977).

Kelley, A., Harbison, W., and Belz, H.. *The American Constitution* (New York, Norton, 1983).

Kendrick, Benjamin. *The Journal of the Joint Committee of Fifteen on Reconstruction* (New York, Columbia University Press, 1914).

Lacy, Dan. *The White Use of Blacks in America* (New York, Atheneum, 1972).

Levy, Leonard. *Judgments: Essays on American Constitutional History* (Chicago, Quadrangle Books, 1972).

Lusky, Louis. *By What Right?* (Charlottesville, Michie, 1975).

Morison, S. E. *The Oxford History of the American People* (Oxford, Oxford University Press, 1965).

———, and Commager, H. S. *The Growth of the American Republic* (4th ed., New York, Oxford Press, 1952).

Morley, John. *Edmund Burke: An Historical Study* (New York, Harper, 1879).

Paludan, Phillip. *A Covenant With Death* (Urbana, University of Illinois Press, 1975).

Rehnquist, William H. *The Supreme Court: How It Was, How It Is* (New York, Morrow, 1987)

Roosevelt and Felix Frankfurter: Their Correspondence, 1928–1945 M. Freedman, ed. (Boston, Little Brown, 1967).

Story, Joseph. *Commentaries on the Constitution of the United States* (5th ed., Boston, Little Brown, 1905).

de Tocqueville, Alexis. *Democracy in America* (New York, Colonial Press, 1900).

tenBroek, Jacobus. *Equal Under Law* (London, Collier Books, 1965).

Woodward, C. Vann. *The Burden of Southern History* (Baton Rouge, Louisiana State University Press, 1960).

ARTICLES

Bator, Paul. "Some Thoughts on Applied Federalism," 6 Harvard Journal of Law and Public Policy 51 (1982).

Bell, Derrick. "Book Review," 76 Columbia Law Review 350 (1976).

Beloff, Max. "Book Review," The Times (London), April 7, 1978 (Higher Education Supplement).

Berger, Raoul. "Constructive Contempt: A Post-Mortem," 9 University of Chicago Law Review 602 (1942).

———. "'Law of the Land' Reconsidered," 74 Northwestern University Law Review 1 (1979).

———. "'Government by Judiciary': Judge Gibbons' Argument Ad Hominem," 59 Boston University Law Review 783 (1979).

———. "Soifer to the Rescue of Legal History," 32 South Carolina Law Review 427 (1981).

———. "Incorporation of the Bill of Rights in the Fourteenth Amendment," 42 Ohio State Law Review 435 (1981).

———. "Incorporation of the Bill of Rights in the Fourteenth Amendment: A Reply to Michael Curtis' Response," 44 Ohio State Law Journal 1 (1983).

Bickel, Alexander. "Book Review," 75 American Historical Review 1509 (1970).

Bond, James E. "The Original Understanding of the Fourteenth Amendment in Illinois, Ohio and Pennsylvania," 18 Akron Law Review 435 (1985).

Bork, Robert. Foreword, in Gary L. McDowell, *The Constitution and Contemporary Legal Theory* (Cumberland, Va., Center for Judicial Studies (1985).

Brest, Paul. "Berger v. Brown et al.," New York Times, December 11, 1977, Book Review Section 11.

———. "The Fundamental Rights Controversy: The Essential Contradiction of Normative Scholarship," 90 Yale Law Journal 1063 (1981).

Crosskey, William. "Charles Fairman's 'Legislative History' and the Constitutional Limitations on State Authority," 22 University of Chicago Law Review 25 (1954).

Curtis, Charles. "Review and Majority Rule," in E. Cahn, ed. *Supreme Court and Supreme Rule* (Bloomington, University of Indiana Press, 1954).

Curtis, Michael. "The Bill of Rights as a Limitation on State Authority: A Reply to Professor Berger, "16 Wake Forest Law Review 45 (1980).

———. "Further Adventures of the Nine-Lived Cat: A Response to Mr. Berger on Incorporation of the Bill of Rights," 43 Ohio State Law Journal 89 (1982).

———. "Judge Hand's History: An Analysis of History and Method in *Jaffree v. Board of School Commissioners* in Mobile Country," 86 West Virginia Law Review 109 (1983).

Dimond, Paul. "Strict Construction and Judicial Review of Racial Discrimination Under the Equal Protection Clause: Meeting Raoul Berger on Interpretivist Grounds," 80 Michigan Law Review 462 (1982).

Ely, John H. "Constitutional Interpretivism: Its Allure and Impossibility," 53 Indiana Law Journal 399 (1978).

Fairman, Charles. "Does the Fourteenth Amendment Incorporate the Bill of Rights?" 2 Stanford Law Review 5 (1949).

———. "A Reply to Professor Crosskey," 22 University of Chicago Law Review 144 (1954).

Frankfurter, Felix. "John Marshall and the Judicial Function," 69 Harvard Law Review 217 (1955).

Friendly, Henry. "The Bill of Rights as a Code of Criminal Procedure," 53 California Law Review 51 (1982).

Forum. "Equal Protection and the Burger Court," 2 Hastings Constitutional Law Quarterly 645 (1975).

Gibbons, John. "Book Review," 31 Rutgers Law Review 839 (1978).

Goebel, Julius. "Book Review," 54 Columbia Law Review 450 (1954).

Gressman, Eugene. "Book Review," 1 New Law Books Reviewer 57 (1986).

Grey, Thomas. "Do We Have an Unwritten Constitution?," 27 Stanford Law Review 703 (1975).

Henkin, Louis. "'Selective Incorporation' in the Fourteenth Amendment," 73 Yale Law Journal 74 (1963).

Hyman, Harold H. Federalism; Legal Fiction and Historical Artifact? 1987 Brigham Young Law Review 905.

Kelly, Alfred. "Clio and the Court: An Illicit Love Affair," 1965 Supreme Court Review 119.

————. "Comment on Harold Hyman's Paper," in H. Hyman, ed. *New Frontiers of the American Reconstruction* (Champaign, University of Illinois Press, 1966).

Lowell, James R. "Abraham Lincoln," 28 Harvard Classics 441 (New York, Collier, 1910).

Lynch, Gerald. "Book Review," 63 Cornell Law Review 1091 (1978).

Mendelson, Wallace. "Mr. Justice Black's Fourteenth Amendment," 53 Minnesota Law Review 711 (1969).

Monaghan, Henry. "The Constitution Goes to Harvard," 13 Harvard Civil Rights–Civil Liberties Law Review 117 (1978).

Morrison, Stanley. "Does the Fourteenth Amendment Incorporate the Bill of Rights?" 2 Stanford Law Review 140 (1949).

Nelson, William. "History and Neautrality in Constitutional Adjudication," 72 Virginia Law Review 1237 (1986).

Nye, Russell. "Comment on C. V. Woodward's Paper," in H. Hyman, ed. *New Frontiers of American Reconstruction* (Champaign, University of Illinois Press 1966).

Packer, Herbert. "The Aim of the Criminal Law Revisited: A Plea for a Look at 'Substantive Due Process'," 44 Southern California Law Review 490 (1971).

Perry, Michael. "Book Review," 78 Columbia Law Review 685 (1978).

———. "Interpretivism, Freedom of Expression and Equal Protection," 42 Ohio State Law Journal 261 (1981).

Richardson, H. & Sayles, G. "Parliament and Great Councils in Medieval England," 77 Law Quarterly 213 (1961).

Soifer, Aviam. "Protecting Civil rights: A Critique of Raoul Berger's History," 54 New York University Law Review 651 (1981).

Van Alstyne, William. "Interpreting the Constitution: The Unhelpful Contributions of Special Theories of Judicial Review," 35 University of Florida Law Review 209 (1983).

———. Foreword, in Michael Curtis, *No State Shall Abridge the Fourteenth Amendment and Bill of Rights* (1986).

Wechsler, Herbert. "The Political Safeguards of Federalism: The Role of the States in National Government," 54 Columbia University Law Review 543 (1954).

Warren, Charles. "The New 'Liberty' Under the Fourteenth Amendment" 39 Harvard Law Review 431 (1925).

Woodward, C. Vann. "Seeds of Failure in Radical Reconstruction Policy," in H. Hyman, ed. *New Frontiers of American Reconstruction* (Champaign, University of Illinois Press, 1966).

MISCELLANEOUS

Act of April 19, 1866, 14 Stat. 27.

1 *Annals of Congress* (Gales & Seaton, 1834, print bearing running title "History of Congress").

Congressional Globe, 39th Congress, 1st Session (1866).

———. 39th Congress, 2d Session (1867).

———. 42d Congress, 2d Session (1872).

Index of Cases

Index